THE
PENNINGTON
LECTURES

The Pennington Lectures, 2011–2015

Edited by
JAN STIEVERMANN

Universitätsverlag
WINTER
Heidelberg

Bibliografische Information der Deutschen Nationalbibliothek
Die Deutsche Nationalbibliothek verzeichnet diese Publikation
in der Deutschen Nationalbibliografie;
detaillierte bibliografische Daten sind im Internet
über *http://dnb.d-nb.de* abrufbar.

Supported by
the Manfred Lautenschläger
Foundation

MANFRED
LAUTENSCHLÄGER
STIFTUNG

ISBN 978-3-8253-6623-0

Imprimé en Allemagne · Printed in Germany
Druck: Memminger MedienCentrum, 87700 Memmingen

Gedruckt auf umweltfreundlichem, chlorfrei gebleichtem
und alterungsbeständigem Papier.

Den Verlag erreichen Sie im Internet unter:
www.winter-verlag.de

Contents

Greetings from
Dr. h.c. Manfred Lautenschläger

Donor of the Pennington Award

This volume contains the speech given at the inauguration of the Pennington Award in 2011 and the public lectures of the first four winners of the Award (2012-2015). James William Charles Pennington, the man whose name the Award bears, was a truly remarkable individual in more than one way. When I first learned about Pennington and his connection to Heidelberg University, my *alma mater*, I was moved. I was deeply moved by what is an extraordinary life story. And I was readily moved into lending the support of my foundation to an award in commemoration of Pennington that would honor his legacy.

On the one hand, Pennington's biography shows the horrors of the slave system from within. It forcefully demonstrates the damage that slavery did to the bodies, minds, and souls of millions of Africans. Pennington managed to escape, but in many ways the wounds of slavery never healed. On the other hand, his life story is also the story of a man who never accepted his fate, who fought for his freedom, and had an outstanding determination to make the best out of his own life – against all odds. As a devout Christian, he was also profoundly committed to helping others overcome the effects of slavery, racism, and poverty.

I believe that both of these dimensions of Pennington's life deserve to be remembered and honored. He deserves to be remembered and honored as a historical witness. And he deserves to be remembered as an example of great courage and faith – as the embodiment of values and ideals to which we should all aspire. This is why, when I first learned about Pennington's connection to Heidelberg University I decided to create an award in Pennington's name.

For me the Pennington Award stands for the values and ideals that informed Pennington's work. These are also values and ideals that I hold to be central and which are reflected in many of the projects I support: first and foremost, the furthering of education and scholarship as a means of individual and social progress; the advocacy of human rights and human dignity for people everywhere; practical help for those who are less privileged and suffering from want; and the promotion of mutual understanding and peaceful dialogue between nations, cultures, races, and religions.

The primary purpose of the Pennington Award is to honor outstanding scholarly contributions to our understanding of the history of slavery in the U.S., as well as the history of African-American history, religion, culture, and literature. The Award also honors scholarship that has helped us understand the wider influence of these African-American traditions on U.S. society and culture, as well as internationally, for example, on the development of the modern concept of universal human rights and justice. In so doing, the Award aims to create more public awareness of these important subjects and promote future research in these areas. At the same time, it is my hope that the scholars honored with the Award will help an international audience to think about the wider meaning of African-American history, the African-American freedom struggle, and the legacy of black theologies.

Since its inauguration the Award has brought a group of extraordinary scholars from renowned American universities to Heidelberg. It has been a great privilege to meet them and learn about their work and their perspectives on Pennington. I am delighted that their wonderful lectures are now available in printed form. I am eager to read them again and look forward to the contributions made by the future Award winners.

The Pennington Lectures, 2011-2015

By Jan Stievermann

Introduction

In 2011, the year of the 625th anniversary of the Ruperto Carola, the Heidelberg Center for American Studies (HCA) and the Faculty of Theology of Heidelberg University established the James W. C. Pennington Award. The Award was generously endowed by the Manfred Lautenschläger Foundation. At the inauguration Prof. Manisha Sinha from the University of Massachusetts at Amherst gave a speech that explored the career of Pennington in the context of the transatlantic abolitionist movement.

James William Charles Pennington was born a slave in Maryland in 1807. From early on, he experienced the brutality of "chattel slavery," which treated and traded human beings like livestock. In 1827 or 1828, illiterate and without any financial means, he escaped from bondage and was sheltered by Quakers in Pennsylvania. Just ten years after his escape, Pennington was ordained as a minister after educating himself and studying (unofficially) at Yale Divinity School. Quickly he became one of the leading black voices against slavery in the period before the Civil War. He lectured widely on the abolitionist circuit, supported the defendants in the famous Amistad trial (1839-1841), established the Union Missionary Society, and coordinated Underground Railroad activities in several communities. To support the cause of abolition, he also published his autobiography, *The Fugitive Blacksmith,* in 1849.[1] This text was very important for the formation of African American literature, and also influenced white authors such as Mark Twain.

[1] *The Fugitive Blacksmith; or, Events in the History of James W. C. Pennington, Pastor of a Presbyterian Church, New York, Formerly a Slave in the State of Maryland, United States* (London: Charles Gilpin, 1849)

The main goal of Pennington's powerful book was to expose the evils of slavery and the underlying "chattel principle."[2] This principle not only exploits the body of the slave, as Pennington writes, but robs him "of his manhood, and transfers his ownership in himself to another," destroys his family, and leaves him without any opportunity to develop his character and potential as a human being.

Due to his early involvement in international anti-slavery activities, Pennington repeatedly travelled to Europe, where, among other things, he spoke as a delegate to the second World Anti-Slavery Convention (1843) and the second General Peace Congress in Paris (1849). In the context of these activities Pennington met the Heidelberg jurist, philosopher, literary author, and liberal political activist Friedrich Wilhelm Carové (1789-1852), who was struck by Pennington's personality, his work as a leader of the anti-slavery cause and by the religious and ethical thought that had informed Pennington's recent autobiography. The same year the book was published, Carové persuaded Heidelberg's Faculty of Theology to confer an honorary doctorate of divinity on Pennington. Just a few months after the democratic revolution of 1848/49 had been suppressed in Baden (the territory to which Heidelberg belonged), the doctorate was awarded to Pennington *in absentia* on December 19, 1849. "You are the first African who has received this honor from a European university," the Faculty wrote to Pennington, "and it is the University of Heidelberg that thus declares the universal brotherhood of humanity." It was very fitting that it was the Faculty of Theology that took this step, for Pennington perceived the fight against slavery very much as a Christian cause. As he wrote: "The gospel rightly understood, taught, received, felt and practiced, is anti-slavery as it is anti-sin."[3]

While Pennington perceived the honorary title as an opportunity to boost the cause, the Faculty of Theology, under Carové's guidance, saw the bestowal of the degree as a sign of recognition for an unusual individual pastor, as well as a form of support for the ideal of universal human rights and a symbolic expression of Western guilt and repentance. As Carové's petition to the faculty reads: "[Europe] has to atone for its terrible and grave guilt for [its mis-

[2] *The Fugitive Blacksmith*, iv.

[3] *The Fugitive Blacksmith*, 76.

treatment of] the wretched sons of Africa who for centuries have been robbed of their most sacred human rights."[4]

At home Pennington continued his fight against slavery and for equal rights both as an activist preacher and as an intellectual. He also continued to work as a teacher for African Americans, who had been denied the chance of a proper education. In his autobiography, Pennington wrote that he regarded this as the worst sin of slavery. He also emphasized "how much now, more than ever, depends upon sound and thorough education among coloured men" to overcome the effects of slavery and racism.[5] For Pennington, an essential part of education was history. Thus Pennington wrote the first-ever *History of the Colored People* as well as significant essays on black emancipation and civil rights.[6] A century before the famous Montgomery bus boycott, Pennington helped to successfully challenge segregated seating in New York City streetcars in the late 1850s. By the time Pennington died in 1870, slavery had been abolished after the bloody Civil War, but it would still be a very long way to go until African Americans could enjoy more equal rights and opportunities in America – although this process is still far from complete.

The James W.C. Pennington Award is given to scholars who have done distinguished work on topics important to Pennington: slavery, emancipation, peace, education, reform, civil rights, religion, and intercultural understanding. The award usually encompasses a month-long stay in Heidelberg to engage in related research and discuss these topics through lectures, seminars and other programs. On the occasion of the award ceremony, recipients offer a public lecture exploring new avenues in their respective fields of research. When the award was inaugurated in June 2011, U.S. President Barack Obama sent official greetings to the HCA to convey his gratitude for the initiative and express his conviction that honoring Pennington's achievements would inspire future generations of Americans and Germans.

[4] Christopher L. Webber, *American to the Backbone: The Life of James W. C. Pennington* (New York: Pegasus Books, 2011), 267-68.

[5] *The Fugitive Blacksmith*, 56.

[6] *A Text Book of the Origin and History of the Colored People* (Hartford: L. Skinner, 1841).

Contributors

Manisha Sinha is the Draper Chair in American History at the University of Connecticut, Storrs. Her books include *The Slaves's Cause: A History of Abolition* (2016), *The Abolitionist Imagination* (co-author, 2012), and *The Counterrevolution of Slavery: Politics and Ideology in Antebellum South Carolina* (2000). She is the co-editor of the series *Race and the Atlantic World, 1700-1900*, from the University of Georgia Press. She has also co-edited the collections *Contested Democracy: Freedom, Race and Power in American History* (2007) and *African American Mosaic: A Documentary History from the African Slave Trade to the Twenty First Century* Vol. I (2004)

The first four recipients of the Pennington Award

2012: Albert J. Raboteau is a specialist in American religious history and was the Henry W. Putnam Professor of Religion at Princeton until his retirement in 2013. His major publications include the pioneering study *Slave Religion: The 'Invisible Institution' in the Antebellum South* (rev. 2004), *Canaan Land: A Religious History of African Americans* (2001), *A Sorrowful Joy* (2002), and *A Fire in the Bones: Reflections on African-American Religious History* (1996). He is the co-editor of *African-American Religion: Interpretative Essay in History* (2013) and co-editor of *Immigration and Religion in America: Comparative and Historical Perspectives* (2008).

2013: Evelyn Brooks Higginbotham is the Victor S. Thomas Professor of History and of African and African-American Studies at Harvard University and was chair of the Department of African and African-American Studies from 2006-2013. Her most significant book publications include the prize-winning book *Righteous Discontent: The Women's Movement in the Black Baptist Church: 1880-1920* (1993) and the new and enlarged version of the African-American history survey *From Slavery to Freedom* (originally authored by John Hope Franklin). Together with Henry Louis Gates, Jr. she is also the co-editor of the 12-volume *African American National Biography* (2013). In addition to the Pennington Award, she won the National Humanities Medal from President Barack Obama in 2015.

2014: Laurie F. Maffly-Kipp is Archer Alexander Distinguished Professor at Washington University in St Louis in American religious history and at the John Danforth Center on Religion and Politics. In addition to researching African-American religions she has also examined Mormon history, religion on the Pacific borderlands of the Americas, and issues of intercultural contact. She is the author of *Setting Down the Sacred Past: African-American Race Histories* (2010) and *Religion and Society in Frontier California* (1994). She has been co-editor of a number of edited collections including *Women's Work: From Antebellum America to the Harlem Renaissance* (Oxford University Press, 2010), *American Scriptures: An Anthology of Sacred Writing, Penguin Classics series* (2010), *Proclamation to the People: Nineteenth-Century Mormonism and the Pacific Basin Frontier* (2008) and *Practicing Protestants: Studies in American Christian History* (2006).

2015: William L. Andrews is the E. Maynard Adams Professor of English at the University of North Carolina at Chapel Hill. His monographs *To Tell a Free Story: The First Century of Afro-American Autobiography, 1760-1865* (1986) and *The Literary Career of Charles W. Chesnutt* (1980) are influential contributions to the field of early African-American and Southern literature. He is the co-editor of *The Norton Anthology of African American Literature* (1997, rev. 2004, 2014), *The Oxford Companion to African American Literature* (1997), and general editor of *The Literature of the American South: A Norton Anthology* (1997). Prof. Andrews is also series editor of *North American Slave Narratives: Beginnings to 1920*, a complete digitized library of autobiographies and biographies of North American slaves and ex-slaves.

Pennington's Diploma

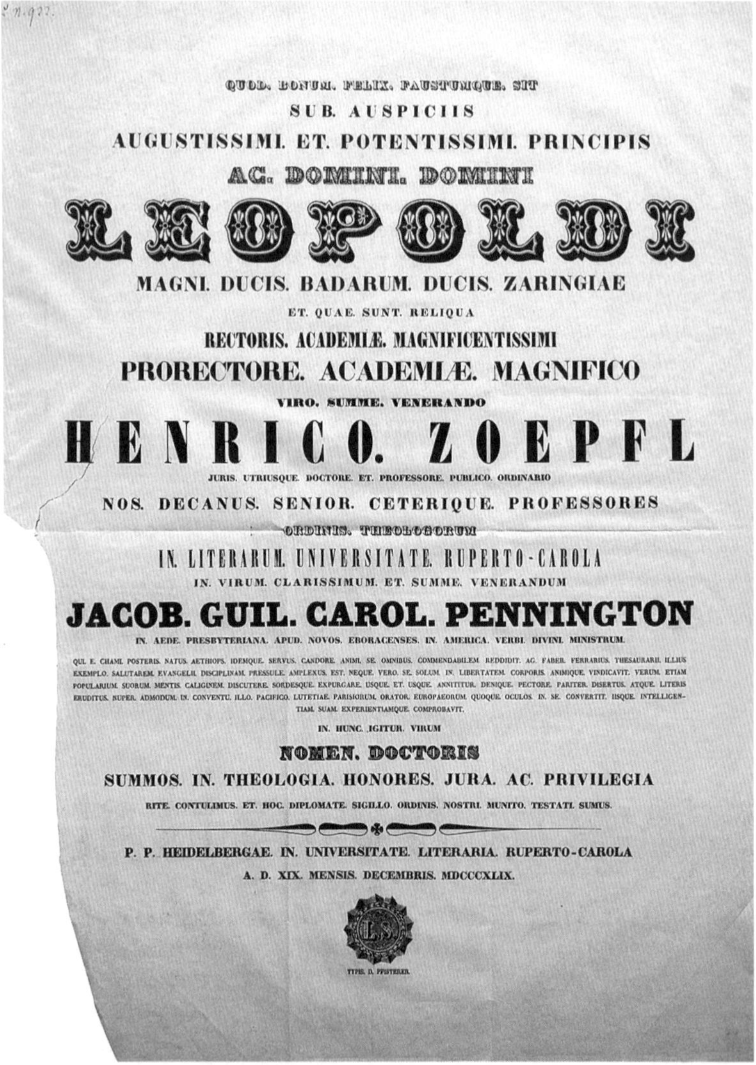

QUOD. BONUM. FELIX. FAUSTUMQUE. SIT

SUB. AUSPICIIS

AUGUSTISSIMI. ET. POTENTISSIMI. PRINCIPIS

AC. DOMINI. DOMINI

LEOPOLDI

MAGNI. DUCIS. BADARUM. DUCIS. ZARINGIAE

ET. QUAE. SUNT. RELIQUA

RECTORIS. ACADEMIÆ. MAGNIFICENTISSIMI

PRORECTORE. ACADEMIÆ. MAGNIFICO

VIRO. SUMME. VENERANDO

HENRICO. ZOEPFL

JURIS. UTRIUSQUE. DOCTORE. ET. PROFESSORE. PUBLICO. ORDINARIO

NOS. DECANUS. SENIOR. CETERIQUE. PROFESSORES

ORDINIS. THEOLOGORUM

IN. LITERARUM. UNIVERSITATE. RUPERTO-CAROLA

IN. VIRUM. CLARISSIMUM. ET. SUMME. VENERANDUM

JACOB. GUIL. CAROL. PENNINGTON

IN. AEDE. PRESBYTERIANA. APUD. NOVOS. EBORACENSES. IN. AMERICA. VERBI. DIVINI. MINISTRUM.

QUI. E. CHAMI. POSTERIS. NATUS. AETHIOPS. IDEMQUE. SERVUS. CANDORE. ANIMI. SE. OMNIBUS. COMMENDABILEM. REDDIDIT. AC. FABER. FERRARIUS. THESAURARII. ILLIUS EXEMPLO. SALUTAREM. EVANGELII. DISCIPLINAM. PRESSULE. AMPLEXUS. EST. NEQUE. VERO. SE. SOLUM. IN. LIBERTATEM. CORPORIS. ANIMIQUE. VINDICAVIT. VERUM. ETIAM POPULARIUM. SUORUM. MENTIS. CALIGINEM. DISCUTERE. SORDESQUE. EXPURGARE. USQUE. ET. USQUE. ANNITITUR. DENIQUE. PECTORE. PARITER. DISERTUS. ATQUE. LITERIS ERUDITUS. NUPER. ADMODUM. IN. CONVENTU. ILLO. PACIFICO. LUTETIAE. PARISIORUM. ORATOR. EUROPAEORUM. QUOQUE. OCULOS. IN. SE. CONVERTIT. IISQUE. INTELLIGENTIAM. SUAM. EXPERIENTIAMQUE. COMPROBAVIT.

IN. HUNC. IGITUR. VIRUM

NOMEN. DOCTORIS

SUMMOS. IN. THEOLOGIA. HONORES. JURA. AC. PRIVILEGIA

RITE. CONTULIMUS. ET. HOC. DIPLOMATE. SIGILLO. ORDINIS. NOSTRI. MUNITO. TESTATI. SUMUS.

P. P. HEIDELBERGAE. IN. UNIVERSITATE. LITERARIA. RUPERTO-CAROLA

A. D. XIX. MENSIS. DECEMBRIS. MDCCCXLIX.

TYPIS. D. PFISTERER.

Translation

Auf dass es gut, glücklich und gedeihlich sei
that it may be good, felicitous, and fruitful

Unter der Schirmherrschaft
under the auspices

des erhabensten und mächtigsten Fürsten
of the most august and mighty prince

und Herrn. Herrn
and lord. Lord

Leopold
Leopold[7]

des Großherzogs von Baden, Herzogs von Zähringen
Grand Duke of Baden, Duke of Zähringen

und, neben Anderem,
and, besides other things,

erhabensten Rektors der Universität
most noble rector of the university

durch den erhabenen Prorektor der Universität,
through the noble vice rector of the university

den höchst ehrwürdigen Mann
the most honorable man

Heinrich Zöpfl,
Heinrich Zöpfl[8]

Doktor beider Rechte, öffentlicher ordentlicher Professor,
doctor of both laws, public and regular professor

haben wir, der Dekan, der Senior und die übrigen Professoren
have we, the Dean, the Senior and the other professors

[7] Leopold I, Grand Duke of Baden (1790-1852); with the territorial changes after the end of the Holy Roman Empire, Heidelberg became part of Baden.
[8] Heinrich Zöpfl (1807-1877), professor of state law at Heidelberg University since 1839; during the revolution of 1848/49 he served as vice rector.

der Fakultät der Theologen
belonging to the faculty of theologians

an der Universität Ruperto Carola
at the University Ruperto Carola

auf den hoch angesehenen und verehrungswürdigsten Mann,
to the highly esteemed and venerable man

James William Charles Pennington,
James William Charles Pennington

auf den Diener an Gottes Wort in der presbyterianischen Kirche zu New York in Amerika, der, geboren aus der Nachkommenschaft des Ham,[9] ein Afrikaner [Äthiopier], und Sklave, sich durch seine Redlichkeit allen als empfehlenswert erwiesen hat; und als Handwerker und Schmied nach dem Beispiel jenes Schatzmeisters[10] die heilsame Unterweisung des Evangeliums eng umschlungen hat und der nicht nur sich selbst in die Freiheit über Körper und Seele gebracht hat, sondern sich auch immer wieder eifrig darum bemüht, die geistige Blindheit seiner Landsmänner zu zerstreuen und ihre verderbte Gesinnung zu reinigen. Schließlich in gleicher Weise vornehm in seinem Charakter und gebildet in den Wissenschaften, hat er vor sehr kurzer Zeit auf dem bekannten Friedenskongress in Paris als Redner sogar die Augen der Europäer auf sich gezogen und hat ihnen seine Klugheit und seine Erfahrung demonstriert.

to the minister of the word of God in the Presbyterian church in New York in America, who, born of the posterity of Ham, an Ethiopian, and slave, has by his integrity proved himself to be commendable; and who, as an artisan and blacksmith after the example of that treasurer, has closely embraced the saving teachings of the gospel; and who not only secured his own freedom of body and soul, but has also continuously been striving to dispel the blindness of his countrymen and purge their corrupt disposition. Equally noble in character and educated in the sciences, he, as a speaker at the famous Peace Congress in Paris, has also re-

[9] A reference to the table of nations in Gen. 10.

[10] A reference to the famous conversion story of the Ethiopian eunuch and treasurer in Acts 8:27-40.

cently attracted the attention of the Europeans and demonstrated to them his intelligence and experience.

Auf diesen Mann also
to this man now

haben wir den Titel eines Doktors,
have we the title of a doctor

die höchsten Ehren in der Theologie, kraft der uns zustehenden Rechte und Privilegien
the highest honors in theology, by virtue of our proper rights and privileges

rechtmäßig übertragen und mit dieser, durch das Siegel unserer Fakultät beglaubigten, Urkunde bezeugt
rightfully bestowed and have attested it by this diploma certified with the seal of our faculty

P.P. ["publicatum/promulgatum] publice"] Öffentlich bekannt gemacht, zu Heidelberg an der Universität Ruperto Carola
P. P. ["publicatum/promulgatum] publice"] Promulgated in Heidelberg at the University Ruperto Carola

im Jahre des Herrn am 19. des Monats Dezember 1849
in the year of our Lord on the 19th of the month of December, 1849

James William Charles Pennington (1807-1870)

James W. C. Pennington and Transatlantic Abolitionism

By Manisha Sinha

I am honored to be invited to celebrate the endowing of an award in honor of the black abolitionist the Reverend James W. C. Pennington on the occasion of the 625th anniversary of the University of Heidelberg. Indeed, the fact that the university has chosen to draw attention to its remarkable bestowal of an honorary doctorate to a black minister, abolitionist, writer, thinker, and former slave in 1849 is extremely gratifying for a historian of abolition and antislavery like me.[1] Today I want to talk about Pennington and the significance of his work but also about the German encounter with slavery and race.

Western Enlightenment thought that stressed universal natural rights and freedom, as well as humanitarian and environmental ideas, formed the ideological underpinnings of antislavery. But as American patriot Benjamin Rush asked: how could Europe "civilized as it is, and thoroughly versed in the laws of nature, and the rights of mankind" have legally authorized "the daily outrages against human nature, permitting them to debase man almost below the level of the beasts of the field?"[2]

[1] On Pennington, see R.J.M. Blackett, *Beating Against the Barriers: The Lives of Six Nineteenth-Century Afro-Americans* (Baton Rouge, LA: Louisiana State University Press, 1982), ch. 1; David E. Swift, *Black Prophets of Justice: Activist Clergy before the Civil War* (Baton Rouge, LA: Louisiana State University Press, 1989), ch. 9; Herman E. Thomas, *James W. C. Pennington: African American Churchman and Abolitionist* (New York: Routledge, 1995); Christopher Webber, *American to the Backbone: The Life of James W. C. Pennington, The Fugitive Slave who Became One of the First Abolitionists* (New York: Pegasus, 2011).

[2] "Benjamin Rush, Address on Slavery, 1773," in Roger Bruns, ed., *Am I Not a Man and a Brother: The Antislavery Crusade of Revolutionary America,*

As far as Africans were concerned, Enlightenment thought was a double-edged sword. While its precepts obviously lent themselves to antislavery use and inspired critics of slavery such as French *philosophes* Montesquieu, Rousseau, Condorcet, Diderot, Voltaire, and the Scottish Enlightenment thinkers Frances Hutcheson, George Wallace, John Millar, and Adam Smith, more than a few made exceptions based on climate, race, and region to their general theories. Viewing the power to reason and write as essential attributes of human nature, ideas associated with the Enlightenment also allowed Europeans to write groups that did not possess an indigenous literate tradition out of humanity. Prominent philosophers from Immanuel Kant and David Hume to G.W.F. Hegel explicitly expressed reservations about Africans' intellectual capacity. For John Locke, while slavery remained outside the social contract, the enslavement of Africans was legitimate, a product of prisoners taken in a "just war." Indeed, Locke's notion of the right to property as a natural right bolstered slaveholders' arguments, but his description of slavery as a state of war lent support to antislavery. The great liberal political philosopher helped write a feudal constitution for the colony of South Carolina, which instituted hereditary ranks and lifetime servitude for Africans.[3]

Racism in the Western world often represented the flip side of loftier ideas on human equality and rationality. These opinions received further backing from the new science of man, which graded mankind along a hierarchical scale in Linnaeus's "Great Chain of Being" that usually ranked Europeans on top and Africans at the bottom. For the cruder racial thinkers of the day they even shared traits with apes and orangutans. The "racist Enlightenment" of Lord Kames (who believed "races" constituted distinct species) coexisted with the environ-

1688-1788 (New York: Chelsea House Publishing, 1977), 224-231. Rush is quoted from p. 226.

[3] See John Locke, *Two Treatises of Government* (London, 1689/90); Charles W. Mills, *The Racial Contract* (Ithaca, NY: Cornell University Press, 1997); C.B. Macpherson, *The Political Theory of Possessive Individualism: From Hobbes to Locke* (Oxford: Oxford University Press, 1962). See also David Brion Davis, *The Problem of Slavery in Western Culture* (New York: Oxford University Press, 1966) and *The Problem of Slavery in the Age of Revolution, 1770-1823* (New York: Oxford University Press, 1999); Henry Louis Gates, Jr., ed., *"Race," Writing and Difference* (Chicago: University of Chicago Press, 1986): Introduction.

mentalism of Comte Buffon and Johann Friedrich Blumenbach. Blumenbach stressed the unity of mankind and varieties within different groups but a simplistic version of his classifications and study of craniums would lay the foundation for scientific racism in the nineteenth century. Blumenbach insisted that Africans were naturally equal in intelligence and mental capacity to Europeans but still saw the latter as "savage" and the former as "civilized." The skull of a female Georgian was his exemplar of beauty. The Caucasian, the original type for Blumenbach, connoted beauty and civilization.[4]

The political heritage of the Enlightenment, like its intellectual legacy, was a mixed blessing for African Americans, giving a powerful impetus to antislavery but also containing elements that justified their enslavement. A commitment to republicanism could range from a conservative belief in propertied citizenship and the political exclusion of the dependent, non-propertied to more progressive ideas of universal liberty and equality and even demands for social justice and economic parity. Racial slavery could act as the material basis for the growth of "white republicanism" in the American colonies. And protection of material and property interests in slavery was as much a cause for rebellion for some patriot slaveholders as ideas about liberty and self-government. But belief in republicanism also posed a threat to slavery, which in turn could weaken commitment to revolutionary ideals. With the start of the American Revolution, which in turn inaugurated the age of revolution in the Western world, all these ideas and the ways in which they shaped the antislavery impulse became evident.[5]

[4] See Johann Friedrich Blumenbach, *The Anthropological Treatises of Johann Friedrich Blumenbach: De Generis Humani Varietate Nativa,* trans. and ed. Thomas Bendyshe (London: Longman, Green, Roberts & Green, 1865) and Raj Bhopal, "The Beautiful Skull and Blumenbach's Errors: The Birth of the Scientific Concept of Race," *British Medical Journal* 335 (Dec 22, 2007): 1308-9. On this subject, see also Nell Irvin Painter, *The History of White People* (New York: Norton, 2010), 41-90, 113-8; Winthrop Jordan, *White Over Black: American Attitudes Toward the Negro, 1550-1812* (New York: W. W. Norton & Co., 1968), chs. 4 & 13; Bruce Dain, *A Hideous Monster of the Mind: American Race Theory in the Early Republic* (Cambridge, MA: Harvard University Press, 2002), 9-26, 59-65.

[5] J. G. A. Pocock, *The Machiavellian Moment: Florentine Political Thought and the Atlantic Republican Tradition* (Princeton: Princeton University Press, 1975); Edmund Morgan, *American Slavery, American Freedom: The*

While most students of transatlantic abolitionism are familiar with the story of the Anglo-American antislavery movements of the eighteenth and nineteenth centuries and more recently, of the impact of the French and Haitian Revolutions on the course of slavery and abolition, they have not paid enough attention to the German story. Even today we know much more about the contributions of German Forty-Eighters to the abolition movement in the United States in the nineteenth century than about the impact of early German antislavery ideas and encounters between Germans and people of African descent like Pennington. On the very eve of the English movement against the African slave trade and the rise of the first wave of antislavery in the early American Republic, the famous German philosopher Johann Gottfried Herder criticized slavery and European colonialism in his seminal *Ideas for a Philosophy of the History of Mankind*.[6] The famous abolitionist slogan "Am I Not a Man and a Brother?" can just as well be attributed to Herder as the British Quakers because Herder had asked, "Is the African not a Man and your Brother?" No doubt, Herder, like Quaker abolitionists, was influenced by the New Testament and the biblical question Cain had raised, "Am I My Brother's Keeper?" Herder's invocation of "Humanitate," which he adopted from Diderot and the French Revolution, also allowed him to develop a trenchant critique of European colonialism, which he described in his poem on Christopher Columbus as a crime against humanity by the "white race." Nearer home, he criticized the German princes who were complicit in the slave trade. While Herder, like many European thinkers of his age, made certain connections between climate and race that promoted

Ordeal of Colonial Virginia (New York: Norton, 1975); David Waldstreicher, *Slavery's Constitution: From Revolution to Ratification* (New York: Hill and Wang, 2009), ch. 1; George William Van Cleve, *A Slaveholders' Union: Slavery, Politics, and the Constitution in the Early American Republic* (Chicago: Chicago University Press, 2010); Donald L. Robinson, *Slavery in the Structure of American Politics, 1765-1820* (New York: Harcourt Brace Jovanovich, 1971), 54-81; Duncan J. MacLeod, *Slavery, Race and the American Revolution* (Cambridge, UK: Cambridge University Press, 1974).

6 J.G. Herder, *Ideas for the Philosophy of the History of Mankind* (1784-1791). For a recent edition, see *J.G. Herder on Social & Political Culture,* Cambridge Studies in the History and Theory of Politics, ed. F.M. Barnard (Cambridge, UK: Cambridge University Press, 2010).

notions of racial difference as a result of the environment, he was a severe critic of slavery.[7]

In his remarkable cycle of poems, ironically entitled "Neger Idyllen," Herder reversed the symbolism of black and white, good and evil, writing "Der Neger mahlt den Teufel weis" (The Negro paints the Devil white) and referring to the "noble black man" and his master as a "white devil." Also reversing the empty morality of Christianization and colonization, Herder tells the tale of a dying slave: "'Warum gießest du mir Wasser auf den Kopf?' sagte jener sterbende Sklave zum Missionar … 'Ich mag keinen Himmel, wo Weisse sind,' sprach er, kehrete das Gesicht ab und starb." ('Why did you pour water over my head?' a dying slave asked the missionary, 'I do not want a heaven where there are white people,' turned his face away and died.") The hero of one of his poems is a slave rebel, Zimeo, the head of a maroon community of runaway slaves in Jamaica, who vows that his son shall never be a slave to a white man. Another poem tells the story of a slave Fetu, who cuts off his right hand rather than kill a fellow slave. Herder was also aware of the early American abolitionists as one of his poems "Der Geburtstag" celebrates Warner Mifflin, the Quaker abolitionist in Delaware who freed his slaves. Not until the radical German Jewish poet Heinrich Heine published "Das Sklavenschiff" (The Slave Ship) in 1855, would any German write such overtly abolitionist poems. Not surprisingly, Herderian philosophy and ideas were a huge influence on twentieth-century African-American intellectuals and activists like W. E. B. Du Bois, who studied in Berlin and received his *doctor honoris causa* from Humboldt University in 1958, nearly a hundred years after Heidelberg honored Pennington. The German explorer and naturalist, Alexander von Humboldt, after whom the university was named, was also, of course, a passionate critic of racial slavery in the New World. Humboldt apparently was the moving force behind Prussia's abolitionist decree of 1857.[5]

[7] Ingerborg H. Solbrig, "American Slavery in Eighteenth Century German Literature: The Case of Herder's 'Neger Idyllen,'" *Monatshefte* 82 (Spring 1990), 38-49; Dain, *A Hideous Monster of the Mind*, 188-9; Mischa Honeck, *We Are the Revolutionists: German-Speaking Immigrants and American Abolitionists After 1848* (Athens, GA: University of Georgia Press, 2011), 26, 28; Philip S. Foner, *Alexander von Humboldt on Slavery in the United States* (Humboldt Univ.: Berlin, Germany, 1981).

Many German revolutionaries and liberal thinkers of the mid-nineteenth century would express abolitionist sentiments. Heinrich Heine's satirical poem "The Slave Ship" was one of the few overtly abolitionist poems written in German at this time. It has often been overlooked although it was comparable to those written by Anglo-American abolitionist poets like William Cowper and John Greenleaf Whittier. In his poem, Heine delivers a searing critique of European greed, religious hypocrisy, and racism illustrated by a rapacious Atlantic Slave Trade.

> The supercargo Mynheer van Koek
> Is sitting and calculating;
> There in his cabin he reckons the worth
> And profits to come from his freighting
>
> The rubber is good, the pepper is good
> At three hundred barrels we'll set her
> I've gold dust here, and ivory –
> The black commodity's better …
>
> In Jesus' name, have mercy, Lord,
> On the lives of this sinful black chattel!
> If they enrage Thee, don't forget
> That they're as dumb as cattle.

As Mischa Honeck has shown in his recent book, many German Forty-Eighters who immigrated to the United States also joined the abolition and free soil movements against slavery at this time.[8]

The African encounter with early modern Europe predated the German exposure to racial slavery. Even before Pennington, Africans had made their presence known in German academia. African scholars in eighteenth-century Europe, when racial slavery had increasingly become the norm in the Americas, dealt directly with the issue of slavery. In 1729, Anton Wilhelm Amo, whose brother was sold into slavery in Surinam, studied in Halle, Germany, and wrote a Latin disputation on the judicial position and rights of Africans in Europe. He went on to study philosophy at the University of Wit-

[8] Robert C. Holub, "Heinrich Heine on the Slave Trade: Cultural Repression and the Persistence of History," *The German Quarterly* 65 (Summer-Autumn 1992): 328-339; Marian Musgrave, "Heinrich Heine's Anti-Slavery Thought," *Negro American Literature Forum* 6 (Autumn 1972): 91-94; Honeck, *We Are the Revolutionists.*

tenberg and taught at the University of Jena. Unfortunately, only his works of philosophy have survived. In 1747, disillusioned with European racism, he returned to the Gold Coast where he died a few years later and was buried in what is now Ghana. In 1965, Halle erected a statue of an African couple to commemorate Amo.

By contrast, Jacobus Elisa Johannes Capitein, brought to Holland by a Dutch slave trader, in his 1742 Latin dissertation justified the enslavement of Africans on evangelical grounds. When Capitein asked, "Is slavery compatible with Christian freedom?" and answered in the affirmative, he was making a plea for the Christianization of Africans and a claim for their spiritual equality. On the face of it proslavery, his dissertation was also a refutation of the racist idea that Africans lacked a soul and the power to reason, and could not make good Christians. He spent his last years in Africa as a missionary increasingly at odds with the authorities of the Dutch West India Company. The French abolitionist Abbé Henri-Baptiste Grégoire would use the examples of both Amo and Capitein to argue for black equality in his antiracist work *An Enquiry Concerning the Intellectual and Moral Faculties, and Literature of Negroes*, published in 1808.[9]

The experience of Amo thus preceded the unusual awarding of a doctorate to Pennington in 1849. In his plea that the University of Heidelberg grant this honor to Pennington, Professor Friedrich Wilhelm Carové, who had first met him in 1843 at the London General Antislavery Conference and later been impressed by Pennington at the 1849 Paris peace conference, concluded:

> The University of Heidelberg was the first to confer this honor upon a Jew (Spinoza) who was called a lecturer of philosophy; the University was the first in which a chair for natural rights and human rights was founded; may the honored theological faculty be the first who, through conferring this doctoral degree, to a North American, to a mistreated

[9] Burchard Brentjes, *Anton Wilhelm Amo: Der Schwarze Philosoph in Halle* (Leipzig: Köhler & Amelang, 1976); Reginald Bess, "A.W. Amo: First Great Black Man of Letters," *Journal of Black Studies* 19 (June 1989): 387-393; Marilyn Sephocle, "Anton Willhelm Amo," *Journal of Black Studies* 23 (December 1992): 182-7; Grant Parker, trans. and ed., *The Agony of Asar: A Thesis on Slavery by a Former Slave, Jacobus, Elisa Johannes Capitein, 1717-1747* (Princeton: Princeton University Press, 2001); Henri Grégoire, *An Enquiry Concerning the Intellectual and Moral Faculties, and Literature of Negroes*, ed. Graham Russell Hodges (Armonk, NY: M.E. Sharpe, 1997): 76-77, 85-90.

> and despised North American, atone through this man for the sins Europe has contributed to natural and human rights.

Carové, who was also the coauthor of a German proclamation demanding the abolition of slavery, asked the university to bestow an honorary doctorate of divinity on Pennington not just as a symbolic gesture. In his presentation, he was careful to mention some of Pennington's works, his recently published autobiography, his textbook of black history published in 1841, and his 1839 speech on West Indian emancipation. In so honoring Pennington, the university then did not just draw attention to the plight of enslaved black Americans, but also recognized Pennington's works as an abolitionist and Presbyterian clergyman of some repute. When Carové died in 1857, the American and Foreign Anti-Slavery Society, of whose executive committee Pennington was a member, held a memorial for the German abolitionist professor.[10] The doctorate itself encouraged Pennington to write more on emancipation and against slavery in the 1850s, cementing his reputation as an original thinker on the problems of slavery and race in the early American republic.

Pennington, an escaped slave from Maryland, was a pioneering black abolitionist. He had participated in the African-American protest against colonization or the plan to repatriate all free blacks back to Africa, as well as the early black convention movement. He had been involved in the famous Amistad case of 1839 and created an independent missionary society, the Union Missionary Society, which eventually became incorporated into the abolitionist American Missionary Association. Mostly self-taught, he had sat in on theology classes at Yale University and became an ordained Presbyterian minister, ministering in black churches in Long Island, New Haven, and Hartford. He was an advocate of black education, teaching in black schools and writing articles on the schooling of black children in *The Colored American*, one of the first black newspapers published in the United States from 1837 to 1841. Ironically, Pennington, who in the 1850s would have to resign from his church because he was accused of intemperance, was also an advocate of temperance as one of the founders of the Colored American

[10] Thomas, *James W.C. Pennington*, 179-186; Mischa Honeck "Liberating Sojourns?: African-American Travelers in Mid-Nineteenth Century Germany," paper in author's possession, 4-9, 11-12.

Conventional Temperance Society in 1833 and an active member of the Connecticut Temperance and Moral Reform Society. In his 1839 address on West Indian emancipation delivered in Newark, New Jersey, Pennington advocated immediate, uncompensated abolition. Like most black abolitionists, he combined reform efforts geared towards racial uplift with antislavery activism.[11]

After he took over the ministry of the Talcott Street Congregational Church in Hartford, Pennington established himself as a writer of some repute in abolitionist circles. In 1841, he published *A Text Book of the Origin and History, of the Colored People* to combat racial stereotypes and misconceptions in popular and intellectual circles. The same year he wrote a preface for a collection of poems by a young black teacher named Ann Plato, helping her to publish it.[12] In his book, Pennington sought to write a correct history of black people that would cultivate a "right state of feeling on the total subject of HUMAN RIGHTS." Using the Bible as his touchstone, Pennington refuted proslavery ministers who "not only . . . desecrated their holy profession but they have taken a part of God's word and construed it into a commission to shed the innocent blood of his creatures." He debunked the popular idea that the enslavement of Africans was justified as they were descendants of Ham and cursed by Noah to be slaves and argued instead that they were "properly the sons of Cush and Misraim amalgamated." Claiming ancient Carthage for African civilization, Pennington argued that slavery was a vestige of the "dark ages" of whom the "American slaveholder" was an apologist.

More interesting than Pennington's exegesis of the Bible and ancient history was his systematic refutation of pseudoscientific racism and racist theories derived from the Bible and popular culture. His

11 Swift, *Black Prophets of Justice*, 205-225; "Minutes and Proceedings of the Third Annual Convention, For the Improvement of the Free People of Colour In These United States, Held by Adjournments in the City of Philadelphia, from the 3d to the 13th of June Inclusive, 1833" (New York, 1833): 15-19. Quoted in Howard Holman Bell, ed., *Minutes of the Proceedings of the National Negro Conventions 1830-1864* (New York: Ayer Co Publishing, 1969); J.R. Kerr-Ritchie, *Rites of August First: Emancipation Day in the Black Atlantic World* (Baton Rouge, LA: Louisiana University Press, 2007).

12 Ann Plato, *Essays; Including Biographies and Miscellaneous Pieces in Prose and Poetry* (Hartford, 1841): xix-xx.

"position" was that the "notion of [racial] inferiority is not only false but absurd and therefore ought to be abandoned." He particularly challenged the racist idea that "there is an inferior order of intellect, and that those of this order are radically and constitutionally inferior, so that no means can change that constitution or raise them from that order." Among the "colored men who have distinguished themselves," he cited Amo, born in Guinea, who had received a doctor of philosophy from the University of Wittenberg. And like generations of African Americans, starting with the mathematician Benjamin Banneker to black abolitionists like William Hamilton and David Walker, he did not hesitate to take on the racist views of the author of America's "Declaration of Independence," Thomas Jefferson. In his *Notes on the State of Virginia*, Jefferson's antislavery pronouncements were severely compromised by his acute racism. Amazed that Jefferson could be blind to the stultifying effects of oppression and slavery on black Americans and his denigration of black writers – including the poet Phillis Wheatley and the Afro-British writer, Ignatius Sancho – Pennington astutely wrote that Jefferson had "plainly discovered to the world the adverse influence of slavery on his great mind."

In fact, Pennington, trying to prove himself a truer son of the Enlightenment than Jefferson, argued "that intellect is identical in all human beings" and that intellect is "the great distinguishing point between man and brute creation." And in another allusion to Jefferson and the racist science of his day, Pennington caustically observed that "he who in discussing the nature of man, can stoop to talk about monkies, apes, and ourang outangs, offers insult to the majesty of his own nature, for which he ought to be ashamed." As a devout clergyman, Pennington insisted that intellect was a God-given gift to human beings and that it was both "inconceivable" and blasphemy to argue that there were different and inferior orders of intellect among men. Like most African American abolitionists, Pennington used a religious rationale to argue against the pseudo-science of race and polygenism in particular, revealing that he not only had the better religion but also the better science than his adversaries. No doubt the theology faculty at Heidelberg in the 1840s would have been pleased at his reasoning. In a small chapter, Pennington even ventured into the racial science of his day arguing that difference of color was mainly attributable to climatic and environmental differences, evoking both Buffon and Blumenbach. And he challenged the venerable American patriot, doctor, and abolitionist Benjamin Rush, who had argued that blackness was the result of leprosy, a skin disease.

At the end of his book, Pennington, who was more interested in the social consequences of racism than the pseudoscience of race, went on to develop a systematic critique of what he called "American prejudice against color," thus becoming one of the first American writers to develop a moral and logical argument against racism. He categorized racism as "supreme selfishness," "emphatically ill will," and illuminated its "tendency" towards violence, as illustrated in mob attacks against abolitionists in the 1830s, "blindness of mind" or ignorance, and its resulting vices among whites of "injustice," dishonesty, hypocrisy, "brutish and uncivil manners," and sacrilege. In an interesting reversal of racist ideas, Pennington attributed most traits of racial inferiority to the racists themselves. Racism, according to him, was "carrying the total [American] nation to a state of refined heathenism." In contrast, Pennington portrayed black Americans as superior Christians who must educate, "love and pity" these "men hating Christians." Slavery in the American republic, he acknowledged, was "the fountain of this bitter stream."[13]

Pennington's speeches, many of which were published, also established his reputation as a leading black abolitionist. In his 1842 sermon, "Covenants Involving Moral Wrong are Not Obligatory Upon Man," which he delivered to his all-black congregation in Hartford, Pennington anticipated abolitionist arguments against the Fugitive Slave Law of 1850. Based on Isaiah 28:8, "And your Covenant with Death shall be annulled, and your agreement with Hell shall not stand," Pennington recommended civil disobedience, i.e., disobeying laws and covenants that "binds men to do wrong." This passage would be the very one that the preeminent American abolitionist William Lloyd Garrison evoked in burning a copy of the U.S. Constitution with its fugitive slave clause and calling it a

[13] James W.C. Pennington, *A Text Book of the Origin and History, of the Colored People* (Hartford: L. Skinner, 1841). Quotations from 3, 12, 43-44, 45, 48, 52-54, 56, 74-80, 85, 89. See also Mia Bay, *The White Image in the Black Mind: African-American Ideas about White People, 1830-1925* (New York: Oxford University Press, 2010): 50-52.

covenant with death and an agreement with hell nearly ten years later. Ironically, Pennington was associated with the Tappanite, evangelical, anti-Garrisonian wing of the abolition movement but, when it came to the fugitive slave law and the Constitution, he anticipated Garrison's radical views. In fact, it was Pennington who first argued,

> How many of the laws, oaths, promises, compacts, agreements, usages and ordinances among men, having high sanction; consecrated with great veneration, and baptized with as much solemnity, will be swept away? Such are the laws and compacts, designed to legalize a system of human bondage.

Such, Pennington further explicated, was "the agreement contained in the federal Constitution, on the part of the Northern States of the Union, to deliver over to his claimant, the fugitive."

In calling for civil disobedience and open resistance to the rendition of fugitive slaves, Pennington, a runaway slave who was active in the Underground Railroad, spoke from personal experience. The black minister proved his proposition in three steps, arguing that the fugitive slave clause of the Constitution involved disobeying God and the doctrine of the Declaration of Independence that "every man is born free and endowed with liberty," that it was a "moral wrong" because it was a "SIN TO HOLD MAN IN SLAVERY" and "WRONG TO ADMIT THE RIGHT OF PROPERTY IN MAN," and finally, that fugitive slave rendition "has in the sight of God no obligation" and "IS NOT BINDING UPON THE AIDING PARTY." Pennington developed a closely argued theological rationale against the law. Like all abolitionists he evoked the higher law of God and the Declaration of Independence against slaveholders' championship of the strict construction of the Constitution on all matters relating to slavery. Referring to the George Latimer fugitive slave case in Massachusetts that had galvanized the abolition movement, Pennington closed his sermon calling upon the "God of Liberty," deftly enlisting the precepts of American republicanism, natural rights, and the Bible itself in the slave's cause.[14]

[14] J.C.W. Pennington, *Covenants Involving Moral Wrong are Not Obligatory Upon Man: A Sermon Delivered in the Fifth Congregational Church, Hartford, on Thanksgiving day, Nov. 17th, 1842* (Hartford: L. Skinner, 1842): 4-11, Quotations on 4-7, 11; Blackett, *Beating Against the Barriers*, 48.

Pennington's writings propelled him into the world of transatlantic abolitionism, and in 1843, the Connecticut Anti-Slavery Society selected him as their delegate to the London Antislavery Convention. Like most African Americans such as Frederick Douglass, Charles Remond, William Wells Brown, and Sarah Parker Remond, Pennington experienced his travels as a "liberating sojourn" free from the all-encompassing pall of American racism, whether it was traveling in unsegregated public conveyances or in day-to-day social intercourse. Black abolitionists, however, were hardly naïve or ignorant of the severe class distinctions and undemocratic political systems that characterized most of the countries they visited or the role of European nations and governments in instituting and furthering American slavery. But they did bask in the individual recognition that their talents and cause brought to them in European countries, especially among like-minded circles of reformers and republican revolutionaries. A couple of years later, Pennington took a leave of absence from his church to visit Jamaica and became, for a while, an advocate of emigration to Jamaica. With the death of his wife and the failure to overturn Connecticut's 1818 law disfranchising blacks, Pennington's stay in Hartford came to an end. In 1848, he assumed the pastorship of one of the largest independent black Presbyterian churches, Shiloh Presbyterian, in New York City. The next year he left for another lecturing tour to London.[15]

Interestingly enough, Pennington penned and published his slave narrative, *The Fugitive Blacksmith: or, Events in the History of James W. C. Pennington, Pastor of a Presbyterian Church, New York, Formerly a Slave in the State of Maryland* in London in 1849. Given the language constraints, Pennington experienced his greatest success on the lecture circuit in England, but it was a German university that would bestow formal recognition on his intellectual achievements. During his first visit to Britain in 1843, British abolitionists had been unsuccessful in trying to procure for him an honorary doctorate. In 1850, Pennington, along with black abolitionist and fellow Presbyterian clergyman Henry Highland Garnet, attended the Frankfurt Peace Congress. Garnet recalled fondly the

[15] R.J.M. Blackett, *Building an Antislavery Wall: Black Americans in the Atlantic Abolitionist Movement, 1830-1860* (Baton Rouge, LA: Louisiana University Press, 1993); Honeck, "Liberating Sojourns?"

kindness of his German hosts and Pennington wrote, "Germany stands high in our affections not only on account of her literary fame, but because of the fidelity her sons . . . have ever shown the cause of human liberty." Indeed, Pennington's life and career as an abolitionist is a good example of the cross-fertilization of abolitionist activism through transatlantic networks.

In his narrative, Pennington not only recounted his first-hand experience under slavery, the trials his family passed through, his dangerous escape to freedom, and the assistance of antislavery Quakers who first opened the doors of education to the self-taught fugitive blacksmith. Unlike most slave narratives, Pennington also wrote a brilliant critique of slaveholder paternalism that bears repeating today for historians of slavery who still remain enamored of that idea. The essence of slavery he argued was "the chattel principle," the reducing of human beings to property, marketable commodities. As he put it, "My feelings are always outraged when I hear them speak of 'kind masters,' – 'Christian masters,' – the mildest form of slavery,' – 'well fed and clothed slaves,' as extenuations of slavery; I am satisfied that they either mean to pervert the truth, or they do not know what they say. The being of slavery, its soul and body, lives and moves in the chattel principle, the property principle, the bill of sale principle ..." The chattel principle was not, he argued, an "accidental result" of slavery. "Talk not," he wrote, "then about kind and Christian masters. They are not masters of the system. The system is master of them; and the slaves are their vassals."[16] Published in three editions in 1849 and 1850, Pennington's narrative was an international bestseller in the English-speaking world.[17]

The decade after Pennington received his honorary doctorate, the 1850s, were a time of crisis not just for the American nation at large but also for Pennington personally. During this time, he was active in black abolitionist circles, in the revived convention movement, the fight for equal political rights, and against colonization. The black clergyman fortified his reputation as a leading black

[16] Pennington, quoted in Honeck, "Liberating Sojourns?" 11.

[17] Blackett, *Beating Against the Barriers*, 42-48; Swift, *Black Prophets of Justice*, 247-251; James W.C. Pennington, *The Fugitive Blacksmith: or, Events in the History of James W.C. Pennington, Pastor of a Presbyterian Church, New York, Formerly a Slave in the State of Maryland, United States* (London: Charles Gilpin, 1849): iv-x.

advocate of abolition, now always using the title of Doctor or the letters DD after his name. In 1853, the young black poet Joseph C. Holly, who published his collection of poems "Freedom's Offering" as a "humble" rather than "representative" member of the "oppressed race," dedicated his anthology to "Dr. J. W. C. Pennington, The Friend of Youth, of Learning and of Virtue, The Worthy Representative of an Oppressed Race – The Gentleman, The Christian, and Scholar, This Volume is most respectfully dedicated, as a small testimony of the High Personal Esteem in which he is held by the Author." The same year, Pennington was elected President of the National Council of the Colored People formed by the national black convention. But things soon unraveled for Pennington, who faced charges of monetary wrongdoing by his associates including Lewis Tappan, for compromising on the issue of his church's complicity in upholding slavery by some Garrisonians, and finally of alcoholism by his own congregation, leading to his ouster from Shiloh Presbyterian. In a series of letters published in Frederick Douglass's newspaper, Pennington adeptly defended his religious convictions and his position in the Presbyterian church.[18]

After a short stay at his old Hartford church, Pennington returned to the small black church in Long Island, where he had begun his abolitionist career. In 1856, he delivered a well-known "First of August Address" to commemorate British emancipation on "the reasonableness of the abolition of slavery in the south." Abolitionists, particularly black abolitionists, often celebrated the first of August, the day of West Indian emancipation, instead of the Fourth of July, the day of American independence. In his speech, Pennington presented a catalog of Western emancipation beginning with the end of slavery in the Northern states to abolition in Latin America, the British, French, and Danish colonies. He particularly honored the history of British antislavery, singling out Clarkson, Wilberforce, and Granville Sharp for their work in the "cause of humanity" and the famous Somerset case for launching the abolition movement in Britain. However, Pennington also criticized British emancipation, especially the apprenticeship system in the West In-

[18] Swift, *Black Prophets of Justice*, 265-270, 340; Joseph C. Holly, *Freedom's Offering, A Collection of Poems* (Rochester, 1853): 3-4; Blackett, *Beating Against the Barriers*, 48-53, 63-73.

dies as "no part of the plan of British abolitionists." Gradual emancipation and apprenticing former slaves were in his words "political expedients of the government to appease the planters." Instead, the abolitionists launched a new campaign to end apprenticeship which was successful in 1838, two years before the system was supposed to end. Pronouncing the British "experiment" in emancipation a great success, Pennington called for an abolitionist rally to arms in the United States, "With the Bible and Declaration of Independence for our weapons, we will make a bold push, for the day comes."[19]

By the end of the decade, Pennington had reestablished himself as a prolific contributor to black newspapers like the *Weekly Anglo-African*, leading the fight to desegregate streetcars in New York City, and against the illegal attempt to revive the African slave trade. After flirting with the new emigrationist organization founded in 1858 by his friend the Reverend Henry Highland Garnet known as the African Civilization Society, Pennington emerged once again in the mainstream of black abolitionist opposition to colonization and any scheme to relocate black people to Africa. He embarked on yet another trip to England on the eve of the Civil War and wrote the introduction to the slave narrative of J.H. Banks, published in London in 1861, a distinction usually reserved for prominent abolitionists. Pennington addressed his introduction "to the friends of universal emancipation in Great Britain and Elsewhere," warning that the "American slave power" had "assumed a most serious aspect" as a "great war power." It had initiated one of "the most terrible civil wars" known in the history of nations, which threatened the peace of the entire continent. That "slavery is the primary cause" of the war, he wrote, "no candid man" can deny. For the last thirty years, Pennington pointed out, slavery had been the bone of contention in Congress, the press, pulpit, the courts of law, and schools, "sowing the seeds of discord." Putting the blame squarely on the slave South, Pennington gave a short rundown of the sectional crisis, the controversies over fugitive slaves, and the expansion of slavery into the West. When the North had at last elected as President "a man of

19 J.W.C. Pennington, D.D., *The Reasonableness of Abolition of Slavery at the South, a legitimate Inference from the Success of British Emancipation. An Address Delivered at Hartford, Conn., on the First of August, 1856* (Hartford: L. Skinner, 1856). Quotations from pp. 11-12, 19-20.

known integrity, Abraham Lincoln of the free state of Illinois," the South had begun to prepare for war. The American Civil War, Pennington argued, involved the friends of "Christian civilization" all over the world. The slave power planned to unite the slave-owning regions of the West and extend its dominion to the Pacific.

If slavery was the root cause of the war, emancipation should be its just result, according to Pennington. Of the 12 million people of African descent in the Americas, he pointed out, over 7 million were enslaved in the seceded states and in Brazil and Cuba. Pennington concluded with his "firm belief" that the "descendants of Africa" are "to be free, remain where they are, and eventually occupy the lands they have watered with their sweat and tears. This is distributive justice." America, he wrote, must "let my oppressed people go free" as "her salvation as a nation" depends upon it. He called on all "true friends of America" to rally around the "cause of my suffering race" and reminded them that it was not the slaves but the masters who had brought on bloodshed, war, and broken the Union. Pennington sought to galvanize the transatlantic antislavery network behind the Union war effort long before the Lincoln administration made the war for the Union into a war against slavery. His trip to London, however, ended ignominiously when he was convicted of shoplifting a book from a secondhand bookstore. After the Civil War, Pennington, like many black abolitionists, worked among freed people in the South, and died in Jacksonville, Florida in 1870.[20]

Much of Pennington's abolitionist career had played out on a transatlantic stage; he had achieved great fame abroad that served to bolster his reputation and aided him in responding to criticism at home. And he had deliberately sought out the honorary doctorate from Heidelberg, as the dean of the faculty of theology, professor Karl Bernhard Hundeshagen put it, "not for himself, as for his

[20] Sharla M. Fett, 'The Ship of Slavery': Atlantic Slave Trade Suppression, Liberated Africans, and Black Abolition Politics in Antebellum New York," in *Paths of the Atlantic Slave Trade*, ch. 5; *I am a Witness Against American Slavery and all its Horrors. A Narrative of Events of the Life of J. H. Banks, An Escaped Slave, From the Cotton State Alabama, in America, Written with Introduction by J. W. C. Pennington, D. D.* (Liverpool, Eng., 1861): 3-7; Blackett, *Beating Against the Barriers*, 60-62, 74-84, Swift, *Black Prophets of Justice*, 329.

color, which is represented by him, and which is so deeply disdained in America. From the granting of his petition, he hopes for an impulse in favor of the blacks and the colored in general."[21] In insisting that the struggle for black freedom and equality play out on an international stage and receive an international hearing, Pennington and the transatlantic movement to abolish slavery that he was a part of bequeathed an important legacy for our own times. And I am delighted that Heidelberg has chosen to honor that legacy with this award.

21 Thomas, *James W. C. Pennington*, 181.

Martin Luther King, Jr. and the Civil Rights Movement: Precedent for Religion in U.S. Politics

By Albert J. Raboteau

> "We shall overcome; we shall overcome; we shall overcome some day.
> Oh, deep in my heart, I do believe, that we shall overcome some day.
> We will walk hand in hand; we will walk hand in hand;
> We will walk hand in hand, some day;
> We are not afraid; we are not afraid; no, we are not afraid today;
> Oh deep in my heart, I do believe that we shall overcome some day."

I begin this lecture with the words of "the anthem" of the U.S. Civil Rights Movement as a tribute to all those who participated in the struggle, especially the countless, unsung, "ordinary" citizens, who exhibited exemplary courage, dignity, and grace, as they faced threats of violence, and even death to gain their human and political rights. I do so lest my discussion of Martin Luther King, Jr. reinforce the unfortunate tendency to excuse political inertia by the absence of a similar "charismatic" leader. We must remember that King, as he frequently noted, did not make the movement, rather the movement made King. The major campaigns in Montgomery, Albany, Birmingham, Selma, Chicago, and Memphis, were preceded by years of grassroots organization based on the development of local leadership, institutions, and protest networks before the arrival of King and his Southern Leadership Conference staff.[1] Keeping this caveat in mind, it must nevertheless be acknowledged that King formulated the most eloquent and enduring statement of the religious and political justification for nonviolent direct action to arise from the Civil Rights Movement, drawing upon his biblical background formed in the African-American church and upon his education in

[1] See Aldon D. Morris, *Origins of the Civil Rights Movement* (New York: The Free Press, 1984).

the philosophical and theological traditions acquired at Morehouse College, Crozer Seminary, and Boston University. A major factor in the effectiveness of King's rhetoric was his remarkable fluency in both languages: his ability to cite Amos and Paul in one breath, Plato and Thoreau in the next. Basing the Civil Rights struggle upon the principles embedded in the biblical narratives of salvation history and the founding documents of the American Republic, King demonstrated the moral force of a movement that many Americans saw as merely a political battle between two groups of extremists. He convincingly propounded the efficacy of the sacrifice ("the redemptive power of unmerited suffering") endured by the "martyrs of the movement" for the soul of the nation.

In a prescient essay published in 1943, A.J. Muste, Director of the Fellowship of Reconciliation, predicted that the stronghold of Jim Crow in the U.S. would only be broken by the nonviolent suffering and bloodshed of African Americans and their supporters:

> Thus it is that whenever love that will suffer unto death is manifested, whenever a true Crucifixion takes place, unconquerable power is released into the stream of history. The intuition that says that God has been let loose on the earth when such devotion is manifest is absolutely sound. This is the true road to liberation. Chiefly: mankind must always depend on its minorities, on the downtrodden, to show the way, since the privileged are too much bound by their vested interests ... If the Negro churches of this country were to give the lead to their own people and their friends in the use of this basically Christian way of redemption, it would constitute another great step toward the achievement of a revolution greater and more beneficent than all the revolutions of the past.[2]

Twenty years later Muste's prediction would be tested in the Deep South. On Sunday morning, September 15, 1963, the congregation of 16th Street Baptist Church in Birmingham, Alabama was busy preparing for Youth Day, an annual opportunity to honor the children of the congregation by giving them roles in conducting the service. Sixteenth Street Baptist had served as the rallying point for the civil rights demonstrations that had drawn national, indeed international attention, thanks to the cattle prods, clubs, fire hoses, and police dogs used by the police on demonstrators, many of them children, in the preceding months. It was a hopeful time for the movement.

[2] A.J. Muste, "What the Bible Teaches About Freedom," in Nat Hentoff, ed., *The Essays of A.J. Muste*, 2nd ed. (New York: A.J. Muste Institute, 2001), 284.

The March on Washington, one month earlier, had mobilized thousands of black and white supporters in front of the Lincoln Memorial in Washington, D.C., signaling a national upswell of support for desegregation. In Birmingham, protest leaders and city officials had finally signed a desegregation agreement one week earlier. After Sunday School, five girls stood checking their appearances in front of a mirror in the ladies' room in the church basement. One girl was fixing the sash on another's dress. At 10:22 a.m. a tremendous blast shook the entire church. The bomb was so powerful that the outside brick and stone wall collapsed into the basement. Out of the rubble staggered 12-year old Sarah Collins, calling the name of her sister Addie Mae. Partially blinded and riddled with 21 pieces of broken glass, she was the only one in the room to survive. Four others: Addie Mae Collins, 14, Carole Roberson, 14, Cynthia Wesley, 14, and Denise McNair, 11, all died. As news of the bombing spread across the nation, and around the world, people of all races were moved to outrage by the tragedy. King remembered his immediate response:

> I shall never forget the grief and bitterness I felt on that terrible September morning. I think of how a woman cried out crunching through broken glass, "My God, we're not even safe in church!" I think of how that explosion blew the face of Jesus Christ from a stained glass window. I can remember thinking, was it all worth it? Was there any hope? ... Where was God in the midst of bombs? ... Our tradition, our faith, our loyalty were taxed that day as we gazed upon the caskets which held the bodies of those children. Some of us could not understand why God permitted death and destruction to come to those who had done no man harm.[3]

One week later, King attempted to articulate meaning in the deaths of the four young people as he delivered their funeral oration to a mourning congregation of blacks and whites and a national television audience.

> These children – unoffending, innocent and beautiful ... are the martyred heroines of a holy crusade for freedom and human dignity. So they have something to say to us in their death ... They have something to say to every minister of the gospel who has remained silent behind the safe security of stained-glass windows. They have something to say to every politician who has fed his constituents the stale bread of hatred

[3] Quoted in Taylor Branch, *Parting the Waters: America in the King Years* (New York: Simon and Schuster, 1988), 889-92.

> and spoiled meat of racism . . . They have something to say to every Negro who passively accepts the evil system of segregation, and stands on the sidelines in the midst of a mighty struggle for justice. They have something to say to each of us, black and white alike, that we must substitute courage for caution. They say to us that we must be concerned not merely about who murdered them, but about the system, the way of life, and the philosophy which produced the murderers. Their death says to us that we must work passionately and unrelentingly to make the American dream a reality. So they did not die in vain. God still has a way of wringing good out of evil. History has proven over and over again that unmerited suffering is redemptive. The innocent blood of these little girls may well serve as the redemptive force that will bring new light to this dark city . . . So in spite of the darkness of this hour we must not despair. We must not become bitter; nor must we harbor the desire to retaliate with violence. We must not lose faith in our white brothers. Somehow we must believe that the most misguided among them can learn to respect the dignity and worth of all human personality.[4]

Coincidentally, the Sunday school lesson at 16th Street Baptist the day of the bombing was "The Love That Forgives."

On June 6, 1965, a new stained glass window was unveiled in the 16th Street Baptist Church. In the worldwide outpouring of grief and sympathy that followed the deaths of Denise McNair, Addie Mae Collins, Carole Robertson and Cynthia Wesley, the people of Wales donated a new window to replace the one of Christ shattered by the bomb blast. In the new window, the crucified figure of a black Christ was depicted, his left hand raised in protest and his right hand extended in reconciliation. The inscription beneath the figure read "You Do It to Me," alluding in light and color to the words of Christ: "What you do to the least of these, you do to me."[5]

The notions of citizen sacrifice and nonviolent protest were intertwined for both Muste and King, as methods of moving the con-

[4] James M. Washington, ed. *A Testament of Hope: The Essential Writings and Speeches of Martin Luther King, Jr.* (San Francisco: HarperCollins Paperback Edition, 1991), 221-23.

[5] Justice came more slowly, however. Four Klansmen were identified as the main suspects in the bombing. Eventually, three were brought to trial: one, Herman Frank, died in 1994. Robert Chambliss, who placed the bomb, was convicted of murder in 1977 by an Alabama court and died a decade later in jail; Thomas Blanton Jr. was found guilty in 2001. And Bobby Frank Cherry, at the age of 71, was convicted of murder by a jury of nine whites and three blacks in 2002.

science of the oppressors and the "guilty bystanders" to empathize with the oppressed and to act to change the entrenched legal structure of white supremacy. The notion of sacrifice for the nation is, of course, a well-established description of military service. The Civil Rights Movement exemplified the sacrifice of civilians for the basic principle of democracy: justice and freedom for all. Just like those willing to die for these values on foreign shores, here were citizens, including even children, willing to die for them at home.

As King (echoing Thoreau and Gandhi) outlined it, nonviolence required active resistance to evil instead of passivity; it sought to convert, not to defeat, the opponent; it was directed against evil, not against persons; it avoided internal violence, such as hatred or bitterness, as much as external violence, because hatred depersonalized the individual. Nonviolence, according to King, was based upon the belief that acceptance of suffering was redemptive, because suffering could transform both the sufferer and the oppressor. It was based upon loving others regardless of worth or merit. It was based upon the realization that all human beings are interrelated. Finally, it was grounded in the confidence that justice would, in the end, triumph over injustice. The hopeful refrain, "The arc of the universe bends slowly but it bends towards justice," which King repeated so often, became a mantra. The belief that suffering was redemptive was crucial to King as the rationale for nonviolent direct action. By accepting the violence of the oppressor, without retaliation and even without hatred, the demonstrators, he insisted, could transform the oppressor's heart.[6]

The deaths in Birmingham were neither the first nor would they be the last of the Civil Rights Era. The reaction of the public to the unmerited suffering of black citizens as dramatized in the public arena by civil rights protestors is one indication of the effectiveness of black protest in changing the minds and hearts of some Americans. Perhaps the greatest demonstration of national action in reaction to racist-inspired violence against peaceful protestors for civil rights occurred two years after Birmingham.

In January 1965, African American residents of Selma, Alabama, and surrounding "black belt" counties took the first steps in

[6] Martin Luther King, Jr. *Stride Toward Freedom: The Montgomery Story* (New York: Harper and Row, 1958), 101-107.

a campaign to gain the right to vote, a right denied them by a system of apartheid that had prevailed in Alabama for as long as they could remember. Mobilized by civil rights workers from the Southern Christian Leadership Conference (SCLC) and the Student Non-violent Coordinating Committee (SNCC), increasing numbers of local black people risked their jobs, their homes, their physical safety, and their very lives merely to register to vote. Rejected time and again by white registrars, they joined together in marches and peaceful demonstrations to protest their disenfranchisement, a persistent reminder of the intransigent rule of white supremacy.[7]

On February 17, Alabama state troopers, wielding billy clubs, attacked a group of marchers in nearby Marion. "Negroes could be heard screaming and loud whacks rang through the square," reported a newspaper correspondent from the scene. When 26 year-old Jimmie Lee Jackson rushed to protect his mother, Viola, and his 82-year-old grandfather, Cager Lee, from being beaten, a trooper shot him twice in the stomach. He was taken to Good Samaritan Hospital in Selma where he died on February 26. In response to Jackson's death, SCLC leaders conceived a plan to march from Selma to the state capitol of Montgomery, a distance of fifty-four miles. On Sunday, March 7, a group of marchers started across the Edmund Pettus Bridge toward Route 80, the highway to Montgomery. On the bridge they were met by a large contingent of Alabama State troopers and local police. After warning the marchers to disperse, the police charged the crowd, releasing tear gas and beating people senseless with billy clubs. Televised on the evening news, images of "Bloody Sunday," as the event came to be known, stirred widespread shame and anger. King issued a nationwide call for religious and civic leaders to come to Selma to participate in another march, scheduled for Tuesday, March 9.

Among the hundreds of clergy responding to King's invitation was Reverend James Reeb, a 38 year-old Unitarian minister who

[7] The following account of the Selma campaign is drawn from Taylor Branch, *At Canaan's Edge: America in the King Years, 1965-68* (New York: Simon and Schuster, 2006); Charles E. Fager, *Selma 1965: The March That Changed the South* (Fayetteville, NC: Kimo Press, 2005); Sheyann Webb and Rachel West Nelson, *Selma, Lord, Selma: Childhood Memories of the Civil-Rights Days* (Tuscaloosa, AL: The University of Alabama Press, 1980); Gustav Niebuhr, "A Civil Rights Martyr Remembered," *The New York Times*, April 8, 2000.

worked as a community organizer for the American Friends' Service Committee in the inner-city neighborhoods of Boston. Reeb not only worked to improve housing in poor black neighborhoods, he insisted on living there as well with his wife and their four small children. The second march was brief. Due to a temporary restraining order prohibiting a Selma-to-Montgomery march, King and his advisors decided to march only to the point of confrontation with the police. Facing the state troopers and police force once again on the Pettus Bridge, the marchers turned and retreated to a mass meeting at Brown Chapel A.M.E. Church. There King asked those who had come from afar to remain until a final decision on the legality of the march to Montgomery came down from the court.

That night Reeb, and two other Unitarian ministers, were attacked by three white men outside a Klu Klux Klan hangout in Selma. Clubbed to the ground, Reeb suffered a massive concussion. His death two days later prompted a national uproar. President Lyndon Johnson went on national television to decry Reeb's murder as an "American tragedy." He closed a forceful speech attacking segregation significantly with the words, "And we shall overcome." In response to the public pressure, the administration finally sent a voting rights bill to Congress. On Monday, March 15, a memorial service for James Reeb was held in Brown's Chapel. Once again King delivered the main eulogy, while distinguished leaders, who had gathered from around the country, also spoke of the meaning of Reeb's death and linked arms to sing "We Shall Overcome" and other movement hymns.

Local black citizens deeply appreciated the presence of white demonstrators in Selma, even though they were keenly aware of the disparity between the national outpouring of publicity and grief over the death of the white James Reeb compared to the sparse attention devoted to the death of the black Jimmie Lee Jackson. Several days after the memorial service, a federal court order was issued permitting the march to Montgomery and the nation watched as white and black Americans joined in the "high water mark" of nonviolent southern protest in the Civil Rights Movement in which people spent five days walking to Montgomery. At the end the crowd had reached 25,000. They gathered at the state house, the symbolic capitol of the old Confederacy.

That movement, described by King, the Roman Catholic monk Thomas Merton, and Rabbi Abraham Joshua Heschel (who marched at Selma) as a *kairos* moment – a time of special divine providence – has served, along with the nineteenth-century abolitionist movement (in which J.W.C. Pennington played an activist role), as a paradigm of religious activism for social justice in the public square. Though many saw it as merely political, King, and those who embraced his vision, interpreted the movement as a moral struggle, a "God-given cause" that moved citizens of different ethnic, racial, and religious distinctions, to act together to form local grassroots organizations and larger national networks in a massive effort to achieve justice for those fellow citizens long denied equal access to "life, liberty, and the pursuit of happiness."

Current distrust of the role of religion in politics is focused upon the divisive force of hot button issues, such as abortion, gay and lesbian rights, school prayer, "family values," the putative "secularization" of American society, the role of the religious right in electoral politics, augmented by the intemperate and emotional, if not vitriolic, language of print, radio, television, and internet commentators, who increase and arouse their audiences by frequently belittling, ridiculing, and demonizing those with whom they disagree. In this atmosphere, comity, trust, civility, and fellow regard – necessary habits for democratic discourse – cannot thrive. Recently, I was browsing in my local bookstore, when two clerks who knew I taught courses in religion, confronted me with an urgent question: "What good does religion do in politics?" They clearly were exasperated by some issue of the so-called "culture wars" featured in the news that morning. As I paused, they added "in 25 words or less." "I don't need 25," I replied. "My answer is Martin Luther King, Jr. and" – remembering the key role of local women in the movement I added – "Fannie Lou Hamer." The two young women were surprised and then nodded, "O.K. but they were exceptions," as if I had cheated. They were, of course, right: King and Hamer were exceptional, but they are exemplary of the values of citizenship which we ought to try to emulate. And both were inspired and motivated by the religious institutions and values of African-American social Christianity. In both historical paradigms of the role of religion in politics – the mid-nineteenth-century antislavery movement and the mid-twentieth-century civil rights movement – whites were enabled to empathize vicariously with the suffering of African Americans through the written or oral witness of escaped slaves or the visual spectacle of modern demonstrations captured in photographs or television (and some in both eras participated directly). This kind of empathetic understanding is crucial to "releasing" the efficacy of the redemptive suffering that King (and Muste) preached. It makes people aware ("I never knew it was so bad"); it troubles their consciences with the dissonance between principle and practice ("How can this happen in America?"); and ideally it leads them to some level of action ("What can I do about this?").

To my mind one of the most empathetic interpreters of King and the Civil Rights movement generally was someone from a very different background than King or those he led. Thomas Merton, a Roman Catholic monk cloistered in a Cistercian monastery in Kentucky, perceived with exceptional insight the historical challenge of the Civil Rights movement and enunciated in a series of rhetorically powerful essays a vision of the state of American democracy that converged with that of King. The coherence of their visions models a kind of communication across differences of racial, vocational, and biographical backgrounds that our current situation desperately needs.

Merton was born in Prades, France in 1915, the son of Owen Merton, an artist from New Zealand and Ruth Jenkins Merton, an artist from the U.S.[8] His mother died when Merton was only six, and his father when he was fifteen. His childhood and adolescence were unsettled. Shuttling between France, England, Bermuda, and Long Island, New York, Merton experienced the homelessness of the expatriate, the restlessness of the transient adrift in an uncaring world, and the longing of the orphan for family stability. Educated at European boarding schools, at Cambridge, and at Columbia between the two world wars, he experienced the disillusionment with the modern world that troubled many of the intellectuals of his generation. His conversion to Roman Catholicism in 1938 incorporated him into a firmly-established system of values that countered the anomie and hedonism he decried in modern society. "Leaving the world," he found both a home and a family in the community life of a strict monastery in Kentucky, Our Lady of Gethsemani.

By contrast, Martin Luther King, Jr.'s childhood was happy and secure. He was born in Atlanta, Georgia in 1929, the son of Al-

[8] Merton's life is recounted in his autobiography *The Seven Storey Mountain* (New York: Harcourt Brace 1948).

berta Williams King and Martin Luther King, Sr., pastor of Ebenezer Baptist Church.[9] Yet although his childhood was comparatively happy, he became aware of the hurts inflicted by racism all too early. Like his father, grandfather, and great-grandfather, King entered the ministry, and throughout the years of his leadership in the civil rights movement, he remained a preacher, regularly occupying the pulpit for Sunday worship, and drawing upon the black church tradition in which he was formed for both the style and content of the political speeches he delivered at demonstrations and appearances in the public square. Courses in philosophy, ethics, and theology at Morehouse College, Crozer Theological Seminary, and Boston University provided King with the opportunity to develop an intellectual framework for systematic analysis of the relationship between Christianity and society, but the existential base for his commitment to social justice was already established in the tradition of black religious protest exemplified by his father's and grandfather's embrace of social gospel activism. Strongly attracted to the intellectual life, King might have combined ministerial and academic careers by choosing job offers at schools in the north, but in 1954 he chose instead to accept the fateful call to become pastor of Dexter Avenue Baptist Church in Montgomery, Alabama.

Our Lady of Gethsemani Abbey and Dexter Avenue Baptist Church represent two very different locations and two very different traditions that nonetheless held a significant trait in common: their marginality. Monks were marginal by profession; they had rejected the dominant values of the world: money, status, power, fame, luxury. African Americans were marginalized by discrimination in a society shot through with the ideology and habits of white supremacy. Both were profoundly extraneous to the priorities and values of mainstream America in the 1950s. Marginality provided both men with the critical distance necessary for radical dissent from the religious and political status quo. Moreover, the contemplative tradition of monasticism and the protest tradition within African-American religion furnished Merton and King with the

[9] For King's life, David J. Garrow, *Bearing the Cross: Martin Luther King, Jr. and the Southern Christian Leadership Conference* (New York: William Morrow, 1986); Washington, ed. *A Testament of Hope*, and Branch's three-volume series, *America in the King Years*, are indispensable.

spiritual insight necessary to articulate convincing critical analyses of society and the religious experience necessary to ground their prescriptions for social change in personal commitment.

Yet it was not their traditions per se, but what King and Merton took from them, or better, the ways in which they were transformed by them, that made all the difference. Initially, neither Merton nor King set out to "save the soul of the nation." There was in the young Merton the enthusiasm of the convert, which led him to espouse in his earlier works, including his bestselling autobiography, *The Seven Storey Mountain* (1948) a world-rejecting attitude that he later came to recant, realizing that "No man can withdraw completely from the society of his fellow men; and the monastic community is deeply implicated, for better or for worse, in the economic, political, and social structures of the contemporary world."[10] We are all, he acknowledged "guilty bystanders."[11] The Merton who had written a series of widely-read spiritual classics suddenly began in 1961 to turn out volumes of essays on civil rights, nuclear weapons, the Vietnam War and expressed radical views on diverse social and political issues. Merton, whose books on contemplation, had continued to attract a wide readership, suddenly spoke out forcefully on national policy issues: war in 1961 and race in 1963. What, many of his readers wondered, did this new "turn toward the world" have to do with spirituality? Quite a bit as one of his most perceptive interpreters argued:

> What had happened to him was that his solitude had issued into what all true solitude must eventually become: compassion. Finding God in his solitude, he found God's people, who are inseparable from God and who, at the deepest level of their being (the level that only contemplation can reach), are at one with one another in God, the Hidden Ground of Love of all that is. This sense of compassion bred in solitude . . . moved him to look once again at the world he thought he had left irrevocably twenty years earlier . . . when he had entered the monastery. He now felt a duty, precisely because he was a contemplative, to speak out.[12]

[10] Thomas Merton, *Seeds of Destruction* (New York: Farrar, Straus, and Giroux, 1964), xiii.rr.

[11] Merton, *Conjectures of a Guilty Bystander* (Garden City, NY: Doubleday, 1966).

[12] William Shannon, "Introduction" in Thomas Merton, *Passion for Peace: The Social Essays* (New York: Crossroad, 1997), 2-3.

Merton had learned that it was the particular task of the contemplative monk, as a man on the margins, to speak out of his silence and solitude with an independent voice in order to clarify for those who were "completely immersed in other cares" the true value of the human person amid the illusions with which mass society surrounds modern people at every turn.

Like Merton, King found his life turned from its expected trajectory, in his case by an unexpected event: the 1955 Montgomery bus boycott, which King neither started nor suggested, but which irrevocably changed him from the successful pastor of a moderately comfortable congregation to the leader of a national movement for racial justice. As spokesman for the boycott, King was overwhelmed by threats against his life and his family. Reaching the end of his endurance, he sat at his kitchen table late one night over a cup of coffee, trying to figure out how to escape his role without appearing a coward.

> And I discovered then that religion had to become real to me, and I had to know God for myself. And I bowed over that cup of coffee. I never will forget it . . . I prayed . . . "Lord, I'm down here trying to do what's right. I think the cause that we represent is right. But Lord, I must confess that I'm weak now. I'm faltering. I'm losing my courage. And I can't let the people see me like this because if they see me weak and losing my courage they will begin to get weak." And it seemed at that moment that I could hear an inner voice saying to me, "Martin Luther, stand up for righteousness. Stand up for justice. Stand up for truth. And lo, I will be with you, even until the end of the world." . . . I heard the voice of Jesus saying still to fight on. He promised never to leave me, never to leave me alone. No never alone. No never alone. He promised never to leave me, never to leave me alone. Almost at once my fears began to go. My uncertainty disappeared.[13]

Both men underwent experiences that widened and deepened their understanding of the paths they had begun. King committed himself to the movement completely despite his growing realization – more certain as the years went by – that it would cost him his life. Convinced that the monk left the world for the sake of the world, Merton devoted himself and his writing, despite public criticism and censorship from his superiors, to trenchant criticism of political issues. Both paths converged initially on the issue of civil rights. Merton, as

[13] Quoted in Garrow, *Bearing the Cross*, 58.

well as King, perceived civil rights as a moral and religious struggle, indeed as *the* religious cause of the day, a view disputed by many Christians who saw it as an essentially secular issue, off limits for a cloistered monk (he was "posing as a white James Baldwin behind the safety of his monastery walls," one prominent critic huffed.)

On the contrary, Merton shared with King a profound belief that in the Civil Rights movement the nation was living through a time of providential testing and opportunity. In the Negro Christian non-violence movement under Martin Luther King's leadership, Merton proclaimed, "the *kairos*, the 'providential time,' met with a courageous and enlightened response. The non-violent Negro civil rights drive has been one of the most positive and successful expressions of Christian faith in action in the social history of the United States."[14]

According to King, the struggle for civil rights presented the nation with an unprecedented historical opportunity.

> The problem of race and color prejudice remains America's greatest moral dilemma. When one considers the impact it has on our nation, internally and externally, its resolution might well determine our destiny. History has thrust upon our generation an indescribably important task – to complete a process of democratization which our nation has too long developed too slowly.[15]

But, both men warned, the moment could be lost, and if it were, the consequences would be dire. The moment, according to Merton will pass without effect and "the merciful *kairos* of truth will turn into the dark hour of destruction and hate."[16]

> The Negro children of Birmingham, who walked calmly up to the police dogs that lunged at them with a fury capable of tearing their small bodies to pieces, were not only confronting the truth in an exalted moment of faith, a providential *kairos*. They were also in their simplicity, bearing heroic Christian witness to the truth, for they were exposing their bodies to death in order to show God and man that they believed in the just rights of their people, knew that those rights had been unjustly, shamefully and systematically violated, and realized that the violation called for expiation and redemptive protest, because it was an of-

[14] Merton, *Faith and Violence: Christian Teaching and Christian Practice* (Notre Dame: University of Notre Dame Press, 1968), 130-31.

[15] Washington, *Testimony of Hope,* 117.

[16] Thomas Merton, *Seeds of Destruction* (New York: Farrar, Strauss, and Giroux, 1964), xiii.

> fense against God and His truth. They were stating clearly that the time had come where such violations could no longer be tolerated. These Negro followers of Dr. King are convinced that there is more at stake than civil rights. They believe that the survival of America is itself in question.... [They] are not simply judging the white man and rejecting him. On the contrary, they are seeking by Christian love and sacrifice to redeem him, to enlighten him, so as . . . to awaken his mind and his conscience, and stir him to initiate the reform and renewal which may still be capable of saving our society.[17]

Why should the "white man" listen? Because, Merton explained, of the authenticity of the black voice, an authenticity born of suffering:

> The deep elemental stirrings that lead to social change begin within the hearts of men whose thoughts have hitherto not been articulate or who have never gained a hearing, and whose needs are therefore ignored, suppressed, and treated as if they did not exist . . . The more the cry of the oppressed is ignored, the more it strengthens itself with a mysterious power that is to be gained from myth, symbol and prophecy . . . The voice of the American Negro began to be heard long ago, even in the days of his enslavement. He sang of the great mysteries of the Old Testament, the *magnalia dei* which are at the heart of the Christian liturgy. In a perfect, unconscious and spontaneous spirit of prayer and prophecy, the Negro spirituals of the last century remain as classic examples of what a living liturgical hymnody ought to be, and how it comes into being . . . where men suffer oppression, where they are deprived of identity, where their lives are robbed of meaning, and where the desire of freedom and the imperative demand of truth forces them to give it meaning: a religious meaning. Such religion is not the 'opium of the people,' but a prophetic fire of love and courage, fanned by the breathing of the Spirit of God who speaks to the heart of His children in order to lead them out of bondage. Hence the numinous force of the . . . art of the American Negro, a force which makes itself felt . . . in the 'Freedom Songs' which he now sings, in the Baptist Churches of the South where he prepares to march out and face the police of states, already frankly Fascist and racist, which arm themselves against him with clubs, fire hoses, police dogs and electric cattle prods, throwing their jails wide-open to receive him. His song continues to resound in prison like the songs of Paul and his companions in the Acts of the Apostles.[18]

Clearly, Merton had read and absorbed King's "Letter from Birmingham Jail." And in response Merton composed poems on the

[17] Merton, *Passion for Peace*, 197-98.
[18] Merton, *Passion for Peace*, 189-90.

children of Birmingham, on the death of Denise McNair, and on the assassination of King.

The concept of *kairos* gave a sense of urgency ("the urgency of now") to their calls for a national renewal that could only come about through nonviolent direct action. Merton shared King's admiration for Gandhi and his philosophy and life of nonviolence. Nonviolence for both was the only method that respected the dignity, indeed the sacredness, of the person. In concert they lambasted contemporary attitudes and behaviors that debased human freedom and deadened human consciousness, especially the mindless striving after power, status, and wealth, and consumerism, which they described as a dangerous collective illusion that effectively reduces persons to objects and relegates interpersonal relationships to manipulation and exploitation. In short, King warned, "we need to move from a thing-oriented society to a person-oriented society."[19] In his essay "Rain and the Rhinoceros," reminiscent of Thoreau's musings on Walden Pond, Merton diagnosed consumerism as a futile attempt to forget our condition of radical contingency, to suppress our awareness of the inevitability of our death. Consumerism works by "creating an illusion of yourself as one who has no needs that you cannot immediately fulfill. Artificial needs are created, typically by mass media, and then 'satisfied,' thus holding out the spurious promise of omnipotence, but actually drawing the consumer into a spiraling cycle of need-gratification-need that can only lead to frustration and end in despair. Trapped in this vicious cycle, we are burdened by illusion and conditioned to suffer all the needs that society demands we suffer."[20]

Merton had no illusions about how powerful a hold consumerism and self-interest held over white America. At the height of optimism in the euphoric aftermath of the 1963 March on Washington, Merton warned how costly the sacrifice would be. He accused white liberals of being ignorant of and unprepared for the radical social change required to effectively solve America's race problem. White Americans, he charged, were primarily interested in profits not persons. A truly radical reordering of priorities was needed. Once made aware of the cost of such change, white liberals would end up

[19] Washington, *Testimony of Hope*, 240.

[20] Merton, *Raids on the Unspeakable* (New York: New Directions, 1966), 15-16.

supporting the status quo. Addressing white liberals directly, Merton claimed that their participation in the March on Washington was not because the Negro needed them, but because they needed the Negro. Actually, their participation blunted the revolutionary impact of the March. In plain and provocative language, Merton took the measure of the liberal's hypocrisy: "North or South, integration is always going to be not on our street but 'somewhere else.' That perhaps accounts for the extraordinary zeal with which the North insists upon integration in the South, while treating the Northern Negro as if he were invisible, and flatly refusing to let them take shape in full view, lest he demand the treatment due to a human person and a free citizen of this nation."[21]

For Merton, as for King, commitment to nonviolence affirmed the preciousness of each human life, an intuition rising out of his own contemplative experience of the presence of God at the still point of each person. "At the center of our being is a point of nothingness which is untouched by sin and by illusion, a point or spark which belongs entirely to God . . . it is the pure glory of God in us. It is, so to speak, His name written in us. It is like a pure diamond, blazing with the invisible light of heaven. It is in everybody. It is the gate to heaven."[22] Likewise, King based his belief in the value of the human person on our common identity as children of God, made in God's image and so worthy of respect. "Every man is somebody, because he is a child of God."[23] The image of God "is universally shared in equal portions by all . . . Every human being has etched in his personality the indelible stamp of the Creator." Thus, if any person is "treated as anything less than a person of sacred worth, the image of God is abused in him and consequently and proportionately lost by those who inflict this abuse."[24]

Human relationship then should be ruled by love – love defined not as affection but as "an understanding, redeeming good will for all." It is an entirely neighbor-regarding concern for others, which discovers the neighbor in every man it meets. King wrote,

[21] Merton, *Passion for Peace*, 163.
[22] Merton, *Conjectures of a Guilty Bystander* (Garden City, NY: Doubleday, 1966), 140-41.
[23] Washington, *Testament,* 255.
[24] Ibid., 119.

> When I speak of love I am not speaking of some sentimental and weak response. I am speaking of that force which all of the great religions have seen as the unifying principle of life. Love is somehow the key that unlocks the door which leads to ultimate reality. This Hindu-Muslim-Christian-Jewish-Buddhist belief about ultimate reality is beautifully summed up in the first epistle of Saint John: 'Let us love one another for love is of God and everything that loves is born of God and knows God.'

Thus, not only acts of violence but internal attitudes, such as hate or bitterness or even resentment had to be abandoned because they contradicted the internal logic of personality and the ordering law of the universe. (How different than the physical violence of the white supremacist then or the verbal violence of the political ideologue today!)

For both Merton and King, the interrelatedness of human beings – the hidden wholeness that binds us all together – is key to understanding and accepting our responsibility for social justice. In King's words, "Whether we call it an unconscious process, an impersonal Brahman, or a Personal Being of matchless power and infinite love, there is a creative force in this universe that works to bring the disconnected aspects of reality into a harmonious whole . . . All life is interrelated. All men are caught in an inescapable network of mutuality, tied in a single garment of destiny."[25]

Belief in our fundamental interrelatedness moved King and Merton to take a universalist perspective on the social problems of their (and our) era. They perceived clearly the connection between the struggle for civil rights in America and the independence struggles of colonized peoples around the world. Earlier than most, they pointed out the link between violence at home and violence abroad, as they insisted upon speaking out against what Merton called an overwhelming atrocity: the Vietnam War. Recognition of the interrelatedness of all persons, they claimed, lays upon all people of goodwill the radical obligation of compassion. Beyond barriers of race, nationality, and religion, we must identify ourselves with the poor, the oppressed, and the wretched of the earth. We must become the voice of the voiceless, the face of the faceless, to an unheeding and uncaring society. This kind of identification, however, if it is to be authentic instead of merely sentimental, requires sacrifice and empathy, not pity.

[25] Ibid., 254.

At the time of King's assassination, mutual Quaker friends were arranging for King to have a visit, short rest and retreat with Merton at the monastery of Gethsemani. The news of King's death devastated Merton. Immediately, he sent a note of condolence to Coretta Scott King. "Let me only say how deeply I share your personal grief as well as the shock, which pervades the whole nation. He has done the greatest thing anyone can do. In imitation of his master he has laid down his life for friends and enemies ... He will go down in history as one of our greatest citizens."[26] Note Merton's encomium of King as exemplary Christian and exemplary citizen.

With extraordinary sensitivity and sympathy Merton listened to the voices of black Americans and tried with honesty and candor to convey what they were saying to white Americans. Seeking to communicate across a racial divide that many whites did not even perceive, he pressed on toward the ultimate end of communication: compassion and community, based upon his own contemplative experience of the hidden wholeness of us all.

The struggle to overcome "the giant triplets of racism, excess materialism, and militarism," as King put it remains arduous. It requires the radical realization that alienation from our true selves, fed and disguised by mass consumerism, leads to violence and to the reduction of persons into things. Contemplation and action need to be joined lest our activism become merely another form of violence and our contemplation another form of self-gratification. Contemplative silence, solitude and simplicity – as Thoreau long ago argued – are necessary in order to come into contact with the true self. But action is also required in identification with, solidarity with, and presence among the poor, the oppressed, the victims of injustice, lest we remain guilty bystanders, obsessed by our desire to satisfy "spiritual" hedonism, no less than material hedonism.

Kairos time may be accurate if it leads to urgency, but misleading, if we use it as an excuse for inaction. "The time has passed: the movement is over." It is not over, unless it is over in our lives. The struggle goes on in local communities across the nation, just as it did before the movement began. Hopeful examples exist in the activism

[26] William H. Shannon, ed., *The Hidden Ground of Love: The Letters of Thomas Merton on Religious Experience and Social Concerns* (New York: Farrar, Strauss and Giroux, 1985), 451.

of the Industrial Areas Foundation chapters and similar networks of organizing for social change that continue to crop up across the nation. Typically based in existing congregations, churches, synagogues, mosques, and temples, the IFA is non-partisan but resolutely political in encouraging local people to meet to identify issues of concern. Citizens are encouraged to speak of their own experiences, to tell their own stories to encourage empathy, and to raise the possibility of imagining change in their lives. Additional home meetings serve to identify and recruit leaders from the community, based on the principle "never do for others what they can do for themselves." Mass meetings are structured to hold public officials accountable for problems of concern. The IAF has fifty-nine affiliates active across the U.S., Canada, the United Kingdom, Australia, and Germany. Their story has been told by my colleague at Princeton, Jeffrey Stout, in his book, *Blessed Are The Organized.* Also on the international level another organization comes to mind, the Sant' Egidio community, which began in Rome in 1968 as a prayer group for peace and which now has branches active around the world in serving the poor and brokering peace agreements among battling opponents, as they did in Mozambique several years back.

The sacrifices of those exemplars in the civil rights struggle must not lie immured in amber in Civil Rights museums, but recalled to life in the many sacrificial acts, small and large, by which we seek to re-member our sundered communities and in James Baldwin's memorable phrase, "achieve our country and change the history of the world."[27]

The Civil Rights Movement exemplifies for us the faculty of empathy, nourished through the telling of and listening to each other's stories, learning and practicing the habits and virtues of citizenship and the democratic process from childhood on. If we hold leaders and each other accountable to their promises and obligations; if we treat opponents not as enemies but as potential allies; if we trust to civil discussion and do not shy away from argument based upon different opinions, values, and religious beliefs that are as important to others as our own are to us; if each listens carefully to each, with respect and forbearance; if we encourage one another in speaking truth to power, no matter the danger; if we keep faith that change

[27] James Baldwin, *The Fire Next Time* (New York: Dial Press, 1963), 97.

is possible; and when we work for it no matter how long and hard the odds seem, then we, like those exemplars we have remembered here, "shall overcome."

I keep returning to one scene in Selma. For me it serves as a simple yet powerful image of the compassion that energized so many to participate in the Civil Rights Movement, a compassion which Abraham Joshua Heschel identified with the divine pathos for humanity that burns like a fire in the prophet's bones. Attending the memorial service for James Reeb were the two little girls, Sheyann Webb, aged 8, and Rachel West, aged 9, who participated prominently in the daily demonstrations. Years later they recalled their responses to the death of James Reeb. In Rachel's words:

> Me and Sheyann used to walk about the church there and look for some sign that would tell us the Lord was on our side, that He was watching us. We'd look and we'd see a leaf falling, and we'd say that was the sign. And we'd know we were winning. We'd see the moon shining down some nights and we'd say that was the sign. And we'd say we were winning. We'd hear the wind blowing or hear the thunder. That was the sign, we'd say. We were winning. So this night, very late, the night James Reeb died, we were out there with all these sad people, and so many of them were still crying. So we walked about the crowd looking for a sign, because we needed that assurance. And we'd heard somebody – one of the ministers or nuns – say that when a good person dies the Lord hangs out a new star in the night. So we looked up for a shiny new star . . . but the sky was full of clouds. And I said to Sheyann, 'There ain't no sign tonight.' And she says, 'Keep lookin' Rachel, 'til we see it.' So we kept standing there, with our heads turned upward like that. And all of a sudden it started raining . . . right in our faces. And I yelled, 'Shey, there ain't gonna be no sign.' But she's still looking up like that and all of a sudden she says, 'The rain's the sign. The rain is.' And I looked up again, letting it just splatter all over my face and in my eyes. The sudden way it had started made me agree that it surely must be the sign. So we sat on the steps of Brown Chapel . . . shivering and praying there. And we were convinced that this rain meant that even the Lord in Heaven was sad by James Reeb's death and He was joining us in our sadness, in our weeping.[28]

[28] Webb and Nelson, *Selma, Lord, Selma*, 117-18.

“Didn’t My Lord Deliver Daniel?”: Biblical Witness and the African-American Freedom Struggle

By Evelyn Brooks Higginbotham

The year 2013 marked two important anniversaries in American history. One hundred and fifty years earlier, President Abraham Lincoln in the midst of the Civil War had issued the Emancipation Proclamation granting freedom to slaves in the rebel states and authorizing the enlistment of blacks into the military. Approximately 200,000 blacks fought to save the Union and to ensure the abolition of slavery in the United States. This year also marks the fiftieth anniversary of the March on Washington. Carrying posters that read “Freedom Now” and “Jobs and Freedom,” more than 250,000 persons of all races and from across the country gathered in the nation’s capitol in August 1963 to demand racial equality through the passage of civil rights legislation outlawing segregation and economic discrimination. I was at that march. I joined with the thousands of others who sang “We shall overcome someday.”[1] I can still remember the words of the freedom songs that we sang. I knew those songs to be the Negro spirituals of the slaves. And thus we clapped and sang, “Oh Freedom, oh freedom over me, and before I’d be a slave, I’ll be buried in my grave and go home to my Lord and be free.” I listened as Martin Luther King, Jr. delivered his “I Have a Dream” speech with an eloquence that will go down in history alongside Lincoln’s Gettysburg address. Reflecting upon the two

[1] See my discussion of the March on Washington as expressive not only of the Southern civil rights movement but of the activism in the North and West in Evelyn Brooks Higginbotham, “Foreword,” in Jeanne Theoharis and Komozi Woodard, eds., *Freedom North: Black Freedom Struggles Outside the South, 1940-1980* (New York: Palgrave MacMillan, 2003).

anniversaries, I cannot help but recognize the role of the Bible and the language of religion in the antislavery movement of James W.C. Pennington's day and in the civil rights movement a century later.

In the secular world of the twenty-first century, we tend not to use explicitly religious language and imagery to the extent that it was used in the past when talking about rights. This is especially the case with progressive social movements. Yet this was not always so. Religious ideas were central not only to the antislavery movement but to the racial struggle for equal rights throughout the nineteenth century and in the twentieth century, certainly during the "long civil rights movement" of the 1940s through 1960s.[2] African Americans included verses from the Bible in the content of their songs, in formal and everyday speech, and in their writings. The use of religious texts often took the form of metaphor and allegory, playing a didactic role in illuminating the meaning of ideas and principles that were abstract, profound, complex, disturbing, and otherwise difficult to comprehend fully. Not least of all, religion motivated people to act and offered guidance as to what form their actions should take.

Calling attention to biblical stories and personalities formed an integral part of black protest politics, and using the Bible in this way proved effective because of its broad recognition by Americans, black and white. Thus, it was common for anti-slavery and civil rights leaders to identify themselves with a biblical figure or be identified by others as such. Harriet Tubman was called the Moses of her people because she repeatedly risked her life to bring slaves to freedom. When Ida B. Wells-Barnett boldly and graphically wrote about the atrocities of lynching in the South in the late nineteenth century, she was identified in religious terms by black people, who likened her to the biblical Queen Esther.[3] In 1963 Martin Luther

[2] In the 1990s historians began to pay greater attention to civil rights activism in the decades prior to the 1950s and 1960s, but the first usage of the concept "long civil rights movement," appears in Jacquelyn Dowd Hall, "The Long Civil Rights Movement and the Political Uses of the Past," *The Journal of American History* 91 (March 2005), 1233-1236.

[3] Kate Clifford Larson, *Bound for the Promised Land: Harriet Tubman, Portrait of an American Hero* (New York: Random House 2004), 53, 136-137, 151, 153-178; for Ida B. Wells as Queen Esther, see Evelyn Brooks Higginbotham, *Righteous Discontent: The Women's Movement in the Black Baptist*

King, Jr. associated his role in the Birmingham civil rights campaign with the Apostle Paul. He wrote in his famous "Letter from Birmingham Jail" that "just as the prophets of the eighth century B.C. left their villages and carried their 'thus saith the Lord' far beyond the boundaries of their home towns: and just as the Apostle Paul left his village of Tarsus and carried the gospel of Jesus Christ to the far corners of the Greco-Roman world, so am I compelled to carry the gospel of freedom far beyond my own hometown."[4] The year 2013 marked the fiftieth anniversary of King's letter.

For more than two centuries the black freedom struggle expressed devotion to Christian ideals and to national ideals, both of which were perceived as affirming human dignity and affirming as well a tradition of freedom to express one's beliefs and to protest. However, in telling the story of men and women whose religious convictions were rooted in Christianity it is important to note that no single religious tradition has a monopoly on the affirmation of human dignity. All the major religions require belief in and devotion to a set of ethical certainties as to freedom and justice, but such moral claims are not limited to the exclusive domain of religion. Moral claims are made by people who do not identify as believing in God. Not all good people are religious and not every religious person is good. And even within a single faith tradition, as with Christianity in America, the Bible was used to argue in favor of slavery as well as to argue against it. In the decades after slavery ended, the Ku Klux Klan committed acts of terrorism against blacks, Jews, and others with the lynch rope and the flaming cross of Christ.[5]

Attention to religious meaning in the black freedom struggle reveals the perceived linkage between the universal ideals in the Bible and the ideals of the American nation as presented in the Decla-

Church, 1880-1920 (Cambridge: Harvard University Press, 1993), 143, 146, 268, fn. 62.

4 Martin Luther King, Jr., "Letter from Birmingham Jail," in *A Testament of Hope: The Essential Writings of Martin Luther King, Jr.*, ed. James Melvin Washington (San Francisco: HarperCollins, 1991), 290.

5 Wyn Craig Wade, *The Fiery Cross: The Ku Klux Klan in America* (New York: Oxford University Press, 1998); Amy Wood, *Lynching and Spectacle: Witnessing Racial Violence in America, 1890-1940* (Chapel Hill: University of North Carolina Press), 153; Manfred Berg, *Popular Justice: A History of Lynching in America* (Chicago: Ivan R. Dee Publishers, 2011), 132.

ration of Independence and the Constitution. African Americans integrated religious thought into their assessments of the law, government, and the authority of rights. This overlapping of discourses, this combining and fusing of religious and man-made principles in the name of God and country constituted an act of sacralization, meaning that the nation and the core principles for which it stands came to represent the sacred. Patriotism after all is a form of religion. However, to "render to Caesar the things that are Caesar's and to God the things that are God's" works best when there is little conflict between the two forms of obedience. All is good, all is just, so argued the advocates of racial equality, when the interpretation and enforcement of laws overlap with religious understandings. But more often than not, because of slavery and the problem of race in America, there existed a fundamental contestation of ideas about justice – a contestation in which both sides (antislavery versus proslavery advocates, or civil rights activists versus segregationists) validated their respective positions by using the same foundational texts: The Declaration of Independence, the Constitution, and the Bible.

The fusion of religious and political discourses was not limited to black Americans. They, like white Americans, perceived a certain amount of divine linkage between the Bible and the founding documents of this nation. This is doubtless true of most eighteenth- and early nineteenth-century Americans. The Patriots of the Revolutionary War, who privileged Enlightenment thought and based their demands for independence from England on the writings of such influential British philosophers as John Locke, spoke in religious terms. In fact, Locke himself inserts religion into his writing. In his *Second Treatise of Government*, published in 1690, this seventeenth-century champion of Reason and individual rights incorporates religious ideas. I am not referring simply to Locke's discussion of humanity in its pre-social condition. On the contrary, in his chapter on the emergence of political societies, Locke draws extensively from the books of the Old Testament. In his chapter on conquest, Locke notes, "I will not dispute now whether princes are exempt from the laws of their country; but this I am sure, they owe subjection to the laws of God and nature. No body, no power can exempt them from the obligations of that eternal law," and he elaborates upon this point through a discussion of the Old Testament book 2 Kings. In his ruminations on legislative power, Locke makes clear the relationship between Nature and God, stating:

> the rules that they [legislators] make for other men's actions, must, as well as their own and other men's actions, be conformable to the law of nature, i.e., to the will of God, of which that is a declaration, and the fundamental law of nature being the preservation of mankind, no human sanction can be good, or valid against it.[6]

In eighteenth- and nineteenth-century America, both blacks and whites perceived God's divine authority as sovereign over man-made laws. Blacks and whites alike interpreted the Declaration of Independence as complementary to God's law. The Declaration admits to a pre-existing, higher authority. First, in its assertion of America as an independent nation among the powers of the earth, the Declaration of Independence refers to a "separate and equal station to which the Laws of Nature and of Nature's God entitle them." Second, in its most quoted passage on self-evident truths, "all men are created equal, that they are endowed by their Creator with certain unalienable Rights, that among these are Life, Liberty, and the pursuit of Happiness." God's law functions as the *Ur*-text, so to speak, for this man-made document, since governments are instituted by the consent of the governed in order to secure our inalienable, natural God-given rights.

Historian Pauline Maier has supplied numerous references to God-talk in the many early state and local declarations in the months prior to the approval of the final text of the Declaration of Independence on July 4, 1776. She does not deny the critical influence of Enlightenment political thought and its emphasis on the contractual origins of government and the right of the people to judge their rulers, yet at the same time she does not disregard the politicized religious language that equated the laws of God with the laws of nature and described self-preservation as "an instinct by God implanted in our nature." Maier tells us, for example, that the people of Rhode Island wrote: "we are obliged, by necessity, and it becomes our highest duty to use every means, with which God and nature have furnished us, in support of our invaluable rights and

6 John Locke, *Second Treatise of Government*, Sections 109, 135-136, 195-196. Also see Jeremy Waldron, *God, Locke, and Equality: Christian Foundations in Locke's Political Thought* (Cambridge, UK: Cambridge University Press, 2002).

privileges to oppose that power which is exerted only for our destruction." The Pennsylvania Conference privileged divine authority, when calling upon "the Arbiter and Governour of the Empires of the World, to witness for us that this declaration did not originate in ambition, or in an impatience of lawful authority ..."[7]

I am arguing, however, that it is not the turn to sacred authority that distinguishes blacks from whites, but rather it is the particular witness in the form of the black interpretation, the black exegesis, and the black hermeneutic that was fundamentally different. While drawing from the same legal documents, the same narratives of liberty, and the same stated precepts of equality upon which America was founded, the African-American biblical witness offered damning testimony as to this nation's ability and willingness to put its democratic principles into practice. In the Revolutionary War era, both blacks and whites found the Exodus story to be explanatory of their situation. Thomas Paine, in his famous and influential pamphlet *Common Sense,* noted the following after the fighting in Lexington and Concord, Massachusetts, in April 1775:

> The blood of the slain, the weeping voice of nature cries, 'TIS TIME TO PART. Even the distance at which the Almighty hath placed England and America is a strong and natural proof that the authority of the one over the other was never the design of Heaven.

Paine – who was a Deist rather than a traditional Christian – then borrows biblical imagery as he continues: "No man was a warmer wisher for reconciliation than myself, before the fatal nineteenth of

[7] Pauline Maier, *American Scripture: Making the Declaration of Independence* (New York: Vintage Books, Random House, 1998), 87-94, 132-156. See also Jan Stievermann, "Defining the Limits of Liberty: Pennsylvania's German Peace Churches during the Revolution," in Jan Stievermann and Oliver Scheiding, eds., *A Peculiar Mixture: German-Language Cultures and Identities in Eighteenth-Century North America* (University Park, PA: The Pennsylvania State University Press, 2013), 209-214. Quoting the declaration of the Lancaster County Committee in May 1775, Stievermann discusses this discursive fusion of duty to God and to nation during the Revolutionary War as involving problematic consequences for the members of Pennsylvania's German Peace Churches, since their religious tenets required that they not bear arms, engage in fighting, or "mix in worldly struggles." Thus, despite their valorization of Liberty, they gave greater primacy to God's dictate as the higher moral law.

April 1775, but the moment the event of that day was made known, I rejected the hardened, sullen tempered Pharaoh of England forever."[8]

For black Americans the Exodus story provided the same vivid allegorical and metaphorical meanings, but in their case it was used to hold the American Patriots just as accountable as King George III. In the same heady times that Thomas Paine was advocating independence from England's Pharaoh and the Virginia slaveholder Patrick Henry was proclaiming "Give me Liberty or give me Death," the Massachusetts slave and poet Phillis Wheatley recounted her own version of Pharaoh in her critique of the political philosophers of the time. In a letter in 1774, she pointed out the hypocrisy of slave-owning American Patriots and referred to them as "modern Egyptians." Wheatley wrote: "In every human Breast, God has implanted a Principle, which we call Love of Freedom; it is impatient of Oppression, and pants for Deliverance; and by the Leave of our modern Egyptians I will assert, that the same principle lives in us ... I humbly think it does not require the Penetration of a Philosopher to determine."[9]

Likewise, in 1776, in the essay "Liberty Further Extended," the black New England minister Lemuel Haynes contended that the Revolutionary War could not usher in true American liberty until freedom was extended to black slaves. Serving in the Continental Army, Haynes based his antislavery argument on the Bible and the Declaration of Independence, when he wrote that freedom was the natural condition of mankind:

> Liberty, & freedom, is an innate principle, which is unmovably placed in the human Species; and to see a man aspire after it, is not Enigmatical, seeing he acts no ways incompatible with his own Nature ... Liberty is a Jewel which was handed Down to man from the cabinet of Heaven, and is Coaeval with his Existance. And ... it proceeds from the Supreme Legislature of the universe.[10]

[8] Thomas Paine as quoted in Maier, *American Scripture*, 33.

[9] Phillis Wheatley to Samuel Occum, printed in *The Connecticut Gazette*, March 11, 1774.

[10] Quoted in Ruth Bogin, "'Liberty further Extended': A 1776 Antislavery Manuscript by Lemuel Haynes," *William and Mary Quarterly* 40 (January 1983): 85-105.

Building upon the rationale of white American Patriots who maintained the right to defy unfair British laws, Haynes distinguished between just and unjust laws regarding the rights of blacks, stating:

> Every privilege [right] that mankind Enjoy have their Origin from God; and whatever acts are passed in any Earthly Court, which are Derogatory to those Edicts that are passed in the Court of Heaven, the act is void. It hath pleased God to make of one Blood all nations of men, for to dwell upon the face of the Earth. Acts 17:26. And as all are one Species, so there are the same Laws, and aspiring principles placed in all nations.[11]

Nearly two centuries later, in the 1960s, with language that is uncanny in its similarity to Haynes, Martin Luther King Jr.'s analysis of just and unjust laws advocated for a moral obligation to disobey unjust laws. Both men were familiar with the writings of the thirteenth-century philosopher and theologian St. Thomas Aquinas. (King is explicit about having read Aquinas.) Importantly, Aquinas himself, in his discussion of just and unjust laws quotes from the Bible, from Proverbs 8:15 ("By me kings reign, and princes decree justice") and from Acts 5:29 ("Then Peter and the other apostles answered and said, 'We ought to obey God rather than men.'")[12]

The Bible offered a moral compass that located a place of special worth for African Americans in a normative universe that included sacred and manmade precepts. The black freedom struggle rested on four explicit principles that have been articulated consistently for more than two centuries and serve as its theological underpinnings: (1) God made humanity of one blood, and this insight is of critical importance because for much of the nineteenth century, black people and white people were deemed different species of humanity, according to science and popular opinion; (2) freedom is a sacred and natural condition for all human beings; (3) God is just and will punish evildoers; and finally, (4) God is merciful to the op-

[11] Bogin, "'Liberty further Extended': A 1776 Antislavery Manuscript by Lemuel Haynes," 85-105; see also John Saillant, *Black Puritan, Black Republican: The Life and Thought of Lemuel Haynes, 1753-1833* (New York: Oxford University Press, 2003).

[12] St. Thomas Aquinas, *Summa Theologica,* see for his discussion of just and unjust laws the First Part of the Second Part, "Treaties on Law," Question 96 "On the power of human Law," Article 4, "Whether human Law binds a man's conscience?" and Article 5, "Whether all are subject to the law?," FS, Q96, Articles 4-5.

pressed and holds in his hands the power of their deliverance, if they will be coworkers with him in that deliverance.

For those men and women who championed the principle of equal justice for all instead of equal justice for whites only, God's law and the law of the land, i.e., the Constitution, needed to be reconciled. They argued that there could be no moral relativism here; there could be absolutely no recognition of the validity of slavery based on property rights law or on arguments about the peculiarities of the Southern economy, or the acknowledgment of slavery's existence in other social and historical contexts. Fidelity to America and its national precepts of freedom and equality, as espoused in the Declaration of Independence, is apparent in the writings of early black abolitionists. Boston-based Mariah Stewart, in a public speech in 1831, articulated this viewpoint: "I am a true born American," she wrote, "your blood flows in my veins, and your spirit fires my breast … The whites have so long and so loudly proclaimed the theme of equal rights and privileges, that our souls have caught the flame also."[13]

Ever present in black abolitionist literature is the recognition that America's democratic ideology fails to ring true and that the Declaration of Independence had been desacralized by white Americans who never fully believed in its stated principles or practiced them. In a speech in 1843 the black Presbyterian minister Henry Highland Garnet discussed the Revolutionary War and praised the Declaration, applauding the document's principles and the eloquence of those who advocated Liberty or Death. He described the words of the Declaration of Independence as touching the very soul of Americans who were, in turn, inspired to fight for what he termed "the holy cause of Freedom." "The Declaration was a glorious document," Garnet wrote, observing that "sages admired it, and the patriotic of every nation reverenced the God-like sentiments which it contained." On the other hand, Garnet was not oblivious to the shortcomings of those same Patriots, and with stinging words he condemned the failure of the Founding Fathers to heed the natural rights arguments that they themselves had championed. "When the

[13] Mariah W. Stewart, "Religion and the Pure Principles of Morality, The Sure Foundation on Which We Must Build" (1831) in *Mariah W. Stewart: America's First Black Woman Political Writer: Essays and Speeches*, ed. Marilyn Richardson (Bloomington, IN: University of Indiana Press, 1987), 40.

power of Government returned to their hands, did they emancipate the slaves? No; they rather added new links to our chains." In the abolitionist tradition, Garnet considered freedom a universal God-given right intrinsic to all of humanity. He stated,

> Unless the image of God be obliterated from the soul, all men cherish the love of Liberty. The nice discerning political economist does not regard the sacred right more than the untutored African who roams in the wilds of Congo. Nor has the one more right to the full enjoyment of his freedom than the other. In every man's mind the good seeds of liberty are planted, and he who brings his fellow down so low, as to make him contented with a condition of slavery, commits the highest crime against God and man.[14]

Garnet's fiery speech was highly controversial when delivered at the National Negro Congress meeting in Buffalo in 1843, since he called upon the slaves to take up arms in large-scale rebellion, just as the American Patriots had done. Equally important, in the mid-1840s Garnet's subversive critique countered the national ideology of manifest destiny, the idea of God's providential plan to broaden the American continental footprint from sea to shining sea.[15] Integral to manifest destiny was the desire for land acquisition through the war with Mexico and for the westward expansion of cotton and slaves.

Henry Highland Garnet was not the first black person to make strong, excoriating pronouncements against the sins of America. Nor was the tradition of religious-inflected warnings unique to black people. In the 1970s Sacvan Bercovitch termed this literary practice the jeremiad, dating it back to the founding Puritans who declared their mission to build their "city on a hill," and who referred to their new homeland in North America, as the New Israel and "the coming of God's earthly kingdom." Like Jeremiah, its biblical referent, the jeremiad warned against the sinful behavior, backsliding, declension, and failure of the people to live up to their

[14] Henry Highland Garnet, "Call to Rebellion: Address to the Slaves of the United States of America," Speech given at the National Negro Congress, Buffalo, NY, August 21, 1843, in *Crossing the Danger Water: Three Hundred Years of African-American Writing*, ed. Deirdre Mullane (New York: Anchor Book, 1993), 117.

[15] Reginald Horsman, *Race and Manifest Destiny* (Cambridge: Harvard University Press 1981), 81-97, 229-238.

covenantal relationship with God.[16] Such behavior was predicted to undermine the community's and the nation's providential role.

Against the backdrop of America as the New Israel, however, African Americans as slaves and as free blacks provided their own counter-narrative. Eddie Glaude and David Howard-Pitney, both scholars of the African-American religious experience, have persuasively argued for the existence of the black jeremiad.[17] In 1829 the black abolitionist David Walker of Massachusetts wrote with apocalyptic imagery as he warned of God's sure and coming judgment on the nation because of slavery: "Oh Americans! Let me tell you, in the name of the Lord, it will be good for you, if you listen to the voice of the Holy Ghost, but if you do not; you are ruined!! When God almighty commences his battle on the continent of America for the oppression of his people, tyrants will wish they were never born."[18] In the 1830s Maria Stewart, who had been a friend and follower of Walker before his mysterious death in 1830, spoke in equally radical terms against the federal government's protection of the slave system. Prophesying God's wrath, she warned: "America, You may kill, tyrannize, and oppress as much as you choose, until our cry shall come up before the throne of God; for I am firmly persuaded, that he will not suffer you to quell the proud, fearless and undaunted spirits of the Africans forever; for in his own time, he is able to plead our cause against you, and to pour out upon you the ten plagues of Egypt."[19]

Frederick Douglass became the leading black Jeremiah in the 1850s. By then, American laws made it necessary for fugitive slaves to flee all the way to Canada for freedom, since escaped slaves any-

[16] Sacvan Bercovitch, *The American Jeremiad* (Madison: University of Wisconsin, 1978, [2012]).

[17] Eddie S. Glaude, Jr., *Exodus! Religion, Race, and Nation in Early Nineteenth-Century Black America* (Chicago: University of Chicago Press, 2000); David Howard-Pitney, *The African American Jeremiad: Appeals for Justice in America*, rev. ed. (Philadelphia: Temple University Press, 2005).

[18] David Walker, *Walker's Appeal in Four Articles; Together with a Preamble, to the Coloured Citizens of the World, but in Particular and Very Expressly, to Those of the United States of America, Written in Boston, State of Massachusetts, September 28, 1829* (Chapel Hill: University of North Carolina, Electronic Copy), 45.

[19] Stewart, "Religion and the Pure Principles of Morality," 40.

where in the U.S. lived in danger of being lawfully captured and returned to their owners. Thus, Douglass had little good to say about America's celebration of liberty. He called the commemoration of the Fourth of July an act of hypocrisy, a sacrilege:

> What, to the American slave, is your 4th of July? I answer; a day that reveals to him, more than all other days in the year, the gross injustice and cruelty to which he is the constant victim. To him, your celebration is a sham; your boasted liberty, an unholy license; your denunciations of tyrants, brass fronted impudence; ... Americans! Your republican politics, not less than your republican religion, are flagrantly inconsistent. You profess to believe 'that, of one blood, God made all nations of men to dwell on the face of all the earth,' and hath commanded all men, everywhere to love one another; yet you notoriously hate, (and glory in your hatred,) all men whose skins are not colored like your own.[20]

While the Declaration of Independence remained popular and was frequently cited by African Americans, the Constitution took on a more problematic character in the years before the Civil War. White abolitionists such as William Lloyd Garrison and Wendell Philips believed the Constitution served slave owners' interests because of its requirement to return runaway slaves, and because of its Three-Fifths Clause, which counted slaves as three-fifths of a person for tax purposes and for Southern representation in Congress. The Supreme Court in the case *Dred Scott v. Sandford* (1857) had gone so far to as to interpret the Constitution to mean that black people, slave and free, were never intended by the nation's founders to be citizens or to be included in "what we familiarly call the 'sovereign people.'" Worse yet, as the Chief Justice Roger B. Taney wrote for the Court, blacks had no rights that whites were bound to respect.

Most black abolitionists continued to believe not in the letter of the law, but in the spirit of the Constitution as expressed in the words of its Preamble, namely, to "form a more perfect union, establish justice, insure domestic tranquility, provide for the common defense, promote the general welfare, and secure the blessings of

[20] Frederick Douglass, "What to the Slave is Your Fourth of July?" (1852), in *Crossing the Danger Water*, ed. Mullane, 157-160. See also David W. Blight, *Frederick Douglass' Civil War: Keeping Faith in Jubilee* (Baton Rouge: Louisiana State University Press, 1991), 117-119, in which he discusses the "millennial nationalism" of Frederick Douglass during the Civil War and in relation to the concept of the jeremiad.

liberty." They believed *that spirit* to be ultimately at odds with slavery. (The words slave and slavery do not appear in the Constitution until after the end of the Civil War, when the Thirteenth Amendment abolished slavery.) With the ratification of the Fourteenth Amendment, which defined as citizens all persons born or naturalized in the United States, and the ratification of the Fifteenth Amendment by which black men were able to vote, the Constitution became a revered document among African Americans. As they saw it, it was not the Constitution, but the judicial system (the judges in local and state courts and the Supreme Court justices) that made a mockery of American democracy and representative government by upholding segregation and disfranchisement laws.

In the early years of the twentieth century, the National Association for the Advancement of Colored People (NAACP) inaugurated the black freedom struggle through the courts and over the decades won victories. As Manfred Berg has written, the power of states' rights over federal law created the need for the NAACP's constant critique and challenge, while using the Constitution itself as a weapon in the fight for voting rights and equal rights.[21] Nor did the challenge to the courts become less relevant after the *Brown v. Board of Education* decision in 1954, which called for school desegregation. Civil rights lawyers continued to represent black plaintiffs and defendants in their pursuit of their rights as American citizens. Even after *Brown,* litigation continued for decades in an effort to provide black youth with the opportunity to gain a quality education or to attend non-segregated public schools in the South and North. It took courage for African Americans to become involved in legal battles in order to attend state universities supported by their own tax dollars, or sit freely on city buses and at lunch counters, or reside in certain neighborhoods, or marry across the color line, or register to vote. It took courage, since the judicial outcome, even when on the side of racial justice, was often accompanied by extralegal activities, e.g., loss of employment, housing eviction, intimidation, and violence.

African Americans' respect for the rule of law and their belief in the spirit of the Constitution are evident in the many civil

[21] Manfred Berg, *The Ticket to Freedom: The NAACP and the Struggle for Black Political Integration* (Gainesville: University Press of Florida, 2003).

rights suits they brought to the courts. However, their faith in the legal system was and continues to be regularly tested and fraught with ambivalence and complexity. This complexity is presented forcefully in the last speech of Martin Luther King, Jr, on April 3, 1968, in a church rally to support sanitation workers in Memphis, Tennessee who were demanding a living wage. In this speech King notified his listeners of the city's injunction against their march, which had been planned for the following day. King informed his listeners, "We're going into court tomorrow morning to fight this illegal, unconstitutional injunction." During this time of Cold War politics, King held America accountable for its standing in the Free World, as he invoked the Constitution in the same way that blacks in the pre-Civil War period had invoked the Declaration of Independence. King stated:

> All we say to America is to be true to what you said on paper. If I lived in ... a totalitarian country, maybe I could understand some of these illegal injunctions. Maybe I could understand the denial of certain basic First Amendment privileges, because they haven't committed themselves to that over there. But somewhere I read of the freedom of assembly. Somewhere I read of the freedom of speech. Somewhere I read of the freedom of the press. Somewhere I read that the greatness of America is the right to protest for right.[22]

It was this mindset toward American law and its limitations that led King's organization, the Southern Christian Leadership Conference, to take as its motto "To save the Soul of America."

The black freedom struggle, as King's remarks reveal, relied on federal laws to fight in the courts while simultaneously looking beyond judges' rulings of constitutionality and unconstitutionality. The emphasis on a higher moral law as the authority for their rights rested on the distinction between God's law and man-made laws. This distinction had been an ongoing motif since the time of black American Patriot Lemuel Haynes in the 1770s. Such a distinction can also be seen in James W.C. Pennington's pre-Civil War autobiography, *The Fugitive Blacksmith* (1849), and in Martin Luther King, Jr.'s "Letter from Birmingham Jail" (1963). In certain ways Pennington is analogous to King. He was a minister, educated, eru-

[22] King, "I See the Promised Land," (3 April 1968) in King, *Testament of Hope: Essential Writings*, 282.

dite, and honored outside the United States. Pennington received an honorary doctorate from Heidelberg University in 1849 because of his abolitionist work, and King received the Nobel Peace Prize in 1964.[23] Pennington helped to organize his community against the separate streetcar policy in New York City in the 1850s, just as King played a key role in the Montgomery Bus Boycott of the 1950s. Also similar is a section in Pennington's slave narrative that is, in effect, written as an open letter to his former master. In April 1963, King wrote from his jail cell words that would become an open letter to the white Christian clergy in Alabama. The "moderate white ministers," as King called them, had criticized the civil rights tactics of Birmingham's black community, prompting King to accuse them of being more devoted to order than to justice.

Both Pennington and King adopted religious and legal imagery in arguing that God stood firmly on the side of human freedom and racial equality. Pennington wrote: "We have the glorious and total weight of God's moral character in our side of the scale," as he warned his former master of the approaching day of Judgment, when they would meet face-to-face at the bar of God. "Sir, I shall meet you there … I have done you no wrong; I have nothing to fear when we both fall into the hands of the just God." Pennington used the phrase God's "righteous moral government" when alluding to international sympathy for the enslaved in America. The entire civilized world, asserted Pennington, questioned whether it was legal to own another human being as property. Pennington believed that the black freedom struggle formed part of a larger, global movement for social justice, as evident in his stated conviction that the "wonderful purple stream, which flowed for the healing of the nations, has a branch for us."[24]

[23] For excellent recent biographical treatments, see Christopher Webber, *American to the Backbone: The Life of James W. C. Pennington, the Fugitive Slave who Became one of the First Abolitionists* (New York: Pegasus Books, 2011); and Taylor Branch, *The King Years: Historic Moments in the Civil Rights Movement* (New York: Simon and Schuster, 2013).

[24] James W. C. Pennington, *The Fugitive Blacksmith: or, Events in the History of James W. C. Pennington, Pastor of a Presbyterian Church, New York, Formerly a Slave in the State of Maryland, United States* (Electronic Edition), 77, 82-84.

A century later King wrote of the superiority of God's justice and also of the international verdict in favor of human dignity. As civil rights activists defied segregation laws through non-violent demonstrations, King stressed the importance of distinguishing just laws from unjust laws. He asserted:

> A just law is a man-made code that squares with the moral law or the law of God. An unjust law is a code that is out of harmony with the moral law ... Any law that uplifts human personality is just. Any law that degrades human personality is unjust. All segregation statutes are unjust because segregation distorts the soul and damages the personality. It gives the segregator a false sense of superiority and the segregated a false sense of inferiority.

Like Pennington, King positioned the African-American freedom struggle within a momentous transnational context – one that linked together, if only metaphorically, as "brothers" the activism of people of color in anticolonial and antiracist movements throughout the world. As King put it, "[the Negro] has been caught up by the *Zeitgeist*, and with his black brothers of Africa and his brown and yellow brothers of Asia, South America and the Caribbean, the United States Negro is moving with a sense of great urgency toward the promised land of racial justice." The urgency for King, like the immediacy of abolition for Pennington, depended not only on recognizing the *Zeitgeist* but also on emphatically rejecting the idea that change comes inevitably with time. Human progress, so King maintained, "comes through the tireless efforts of men willing to be coworkers with God, and without this hard work, time itself becomes an ally of the forces of social stagnation."[25]

It is in this latter regard of being co-workers with God that African Americans' biblical witness constituted more than just prophetic jeremiad and stern criticism of white America. Religious language was effectively used to embolden individuals by strengthening their resolve to make democracy real in America. For two centuries, the appeal to faith stood at the foundation of the call to take courage. And courage was crucial to the black freedom struggle. Bible stories and concepts such as Exodus, Canaan, and the Promised Land had motivated the slaves. They did not revolt in any

[25] King, "Letter from Birmingham Jail," in King, *Testament of Hope: Essential Writings*, 293-297.

great number, although many attempted to escape bondage. For the majority of slaves, religious stories and concepts had affirmed their dignity, when the larger society was denying it. Historian Lawrence Levine wrote that the most recurrent theme in the slaves' songs was that of being "a child of God," even a chosen people.[26] The slaves never doubted their humanity or the "holy cause of freedom," and thus they sang: "Didn't my Lord deliver Daniel, then why not every man. He delivered Daniel from the Lion's den, and Jonah from the Belly of the Whale. He delivered the children from the fiery furnace, and why not a-every man?" At times, such songs mustered the courage to run away – to leave relatives and loved ones behind and to strike out for freedom as the fugitive slave James W. C. Pennington had done. In his autobiography *My Bondage and My Freedom*, Frederick Douglass captured this role of the spirituals for individual slaves. He referred to the joyous singing of songs like "Oh Canaan, sweet Canaan, I am bound for the land of Canaan." Douglass was explicit in noting the double meaning of this song, stating:

> In the lips of some, it meant the expectation of a speedy summons to a world of spirits; but, in the lips of *our* company, it meant simply, a speedy pilgrimage toward a free state, and deliverance from all the evils and dangers of slavery. We meant to reach the *north* – and the north was our Canaan.[27]

If, on one level, the appeal to take courage meant to hold fast to the justness of their cause, on another level it demanded a willingness to put bodies and lives on the line, which in the 1960s meant sit-ins, freedom rides, boycotts, and marches. More than any other influence, religious understandings moved African Americans from a position of prayer and faith to one of moral agency through nonviolent direct action on the ground. Focusing on grassroots activism in Southern cities and in rural areas deep in the southern Delta, recent scholarship has brought to light formerly unknown and unheralded

[26] Lawrence Levine, *Black Culture and Black Consciousness: Afro-American Folk Thought from Slavery to Freedom* (New York: Oxford University Press, 1977, [2007]), 33-34; Albert V. Raboteau, *Slave Religion: The Invisible Institution in the Antebellum South* (New York: Oxford University Press, 1978, [2004]), 320.

[27] Frederick Douglass, *My Bondage and My Freedom*, ed. David Blight (New Haven: Yale University Press, 2014), 222.

men and women at the local level. I cannot overstate the importance of religion to these historical actors. Fannie Lou Hamer, from Sunflower County, Mississippi, successfully rallied her neighbors with appeals to religion. She endured beatings and evictions for trying to register her neighbors to vote.[28]

Deploying the Bible was particularly effective in mobilizing and empowering Southern blacks of low social status and low income to confront powerful whites. Sharecroppers, maids, sanitation workers, along with college students, preachers, teachers, and all sorts of people engaged in boycotts, freedom rides, voter registration, marches, and sit-ins. In the 1950s NAACP worker Ruby Hurley made her appeals through religious language and symbols. She stated:

> I found using the Bible to be effective in saying to our people, 'You go to church on Sunday or you go every time the church doors are open. You say amen before the minister even has the word out of his mouth … Yet you tell me you're afraid. Now how can you be afraid and be honest when you say My faith looks up to Thee or when you sing that God's going to take care of you? If you don't believe it, then you are not really the Christian you say you are.'[29]

Religious imagery figured significantly in the Birmingham civil rights campaign, which entailed a boycott on the part of African Americans of the downtown stores in the months leading up to Easter. This time of year was traditionally a very profitable shopping season for white businesses. However, in 1963 Birmingham blacks refused to purchase any Easter finery and instead marched and demonstrated in protest of segregation. In order to motivate his church audience to action, black Baptist minister James Bevel culled the material for his sermon from the recent past and preached about James Meredith's efforts to register as a student at the University of Mississippi, in the face of the fervent resistance of Mississippi's governor Ross Barnett and the violence of white mobs. Meredith, a veteran of the Korean War, was successful, however, and began his classes at Ole Miss in the fall of 1962.

[28] Chana Kai Lee, *For Freedom's Sake: The Life of Fannie Lou Hamer* (Urbana: University of Illinois Press, 1999), 63.

[29] Ruby Hurley is quoted in Charles Payne, *I've Got the Light of Freedom: The Organizing Tradition and the Mississippi Freedom Struggle* (Berkeley: University of California Press, 1995, [2007]), 273.

Bevel chose the scriptural text for his sermon from the Old Testament book of Daniel, turning specifically to the story of the three Hebrew men – Shadrach, Meshach, and Abednego – who were thrown into a fiery furnace because they refused to obey the law that required them to bow down to the Babylonian King Nebuchadnezzar. He roused his church congregation with a poem that told of Meredith's similar defiance of Mississippi Governor Ross Barnett. In a singing tone, Bevel recited a conversation between the two men, shifting back-and-forth from Barnett's voice to that of Meredith. "Said, I'm a white man, and I have a right to tell you to bow to segregation ... I got mobs and I got sheriffs, and I got gas, bullets and bayonets and guns." Bevel told his audience that Meredith remained steadfast, as he "looked up at Barnett and said, 'Nah, I'm not gonna bow to segregation.'"[30]

Bevel's listeners already knew the outcome of Meredith's efforts to integrate Ole Miss. The story appeared in all the newspapers and on television in the previous fall. His congregation knew, as well, that as civil rights activists they, too, would face hostile, violent opposition in their own city of Birmingham. Confronting them was the Birmingham police force with its guns, dogs, and bayonets. Bevel's black audience most likely thought that their mayor, Bull Connor, hated them no less than Alabama's Governor Ross Barnett hated Meredith. Worse yet, Birmingham had come to be called "Bombingham," because of the many unsolved bombings against blacks in the city, with no arrests made. And yet the black citizens of Birmingham took courage. Those who heard James Bevel's message participated in the demonstrations not only because of Meredith's example, but because they knew well the biblical story of Shadrach, Meshach, and Abednego in the fiery furnace – that the men were not consumed by the fire – just as Meredith had not been killed or hurt, despite the rioting that took place in Mississippi. James Bevel had successfully fused the biblical imaginary with the political realities right there in Birmingham, affirming and inspiring belief in the Lord who would deliver them in their local struggle for free-

30 The poem by the Reverend James Bevel and the discussion of Bevel's impact is discussed in Jonathan Rieder, *Gospel of Freedom: Martin Luther King, Jr.'s Letter from Birmingham Jail and the Struggle that Changed a Nation* (New York: Bloomsbury Press, 2013), 109-110.

dom. The church audience believed Bevel when he told them, "The God that takes care in that day takes care of folks in this day ... The leader of the movement is God himself."[31]

It is difficult to be courageous and to stand up for principles that are unpopular and denounced by the powerful. And it is difficult to take a courageous position when you have no idea as to how your position will be actually received or what the consequences of your actions will entail. But it is even more difficult to stand up nonviolently, as the civil rights marchers did, when they could see vividly the great opposition of violence, imprisonment, and the possibility of death staring them in the face. There are many examples but the Birmingham case is unique in religious symbolism since Martin Luther King, Jr., was arrested and imprisoned on Good Friday. Again, King's "Letter from Birmingham Jail" to the white Christians in the city may be compared with Pennington's slave narrative for the religious ideas conveyed to blacks themselves, and specifically the type of individual and collective self-purification deemed necessary in response to emotional depression and profound disappointment.[32] Pennington referred to the "deep chambers of my soul" and to the great pain he felt for those left behind in slavery. He also expressed the need to address his own personal sins and inadequacies. "I did not by any means forget my fellow-bondmen, of whom I had been sorrowing so deeply, and travailing in spirit so earnestly; but I now saw that while man had been injuring me, I had been offending God; and that unless I ceased to offend him, I could not expect to have his sympathy in my wrongs; and moreover, that I could not be instrumental in eliciting his powerful aid in behalf of those [the slaves] for whom I mourned so deeply."

King, writing about events in mid-twentieth century Birmingham, expressed the same anguish felt by Pennington. He articulated the need for what he called "self-purification," but King conveyed his emotion in a collective voice. The use of the word "self" by African Americans, as in the concept self-help, has always interchangeably meant the individual and the group. More than a hundred years after Pennington, King wrote that

[31] Ibid.

[32] For the quoted material to follow in this paragraph, see Pennington, *Fugitive Blacksmith*, 51-52; King, "Letter from Birmingham Jail," 291.

> our hopes had been blasted, and the shadow of deep disappointment settled upon us … We had no alternative except to prepare for direct action, whereby we would present our very bodies as a means of laying our case before the conscience of the local and the national community. Mindful of the difficulties involved, we decided to undertake a process of self-purification … [and] began a series of workshops on nonviolence, and we repeatedly asked ourselves: 'Are you able to accept blows without retaliating? Are you able to endure the ordeal of jail?'[33]

Despite King's imprisonment, the protest continued. The boycott and protest had emerged organically from the Birmingham community, so local leadership was already in place. Andrew Young, one of King's lieutenants, described in his autobiography the power of religious conviction on Easter Sunday 1963, when African Americans began their march to the Birmingham jail. The plan was to stand outside the prison, to pray, and to sing songs of Easter praise so that King and other prisoners might hear them and be spiritually uplifted. But if this sounds innocent to us today, I assure you that it was deemed a very threatening act, a dangerous thing to do in the early 1960s. Five thousand marchers gathered at the New Pilgrim Baptist Church from which they embarked upon their march, but they got only a few blocks from the jail when they were confronted with a barricade of policemen with billy clubs, guns, and bayonets. Andrew Young described snarling, vicious dogs that stood by the police, waiting to get the command to attack. The civil rights demonstrators, having come from church and dressed in their Sunday clothes, faced firemen poised to turn on hoses filled with gushing, pounding water powerful enough to tear the bark off of trees and to sweep the marchers themselves into the air only to come crashing down. And perhaps most disquieting, the marchers faced the chief of police, Bull Connor, who hated them and the very idea of racial equality. Connor stood at the helm of the barricade, shouting "Disperse and turn around."

Andrew Young recalled this experience, as follows: "[T]o get myself together and as a holding action, I asked the people to get down on their knees and offer a prayer. The entire group dropped to their knees and began to pray. They were praying an old-fashioned kind of long-meter moan, mired with singing." Young stated that

[33] King, "Letter from Birmingham Jail."

while they were praying, he walked ahead to meet with Bull Connor to try to convey that the group only wished to gather outside the jail and sing a few songs and pray. But Connor would have none of this. Andrew Young described the miraculous events to follow in a moving, firsthand account:

> Suddenly, Rev. Charles Billups, one of the more faithful and fearless leaders ... jumped up and hollered: 'The Lord is with this movement! Off your knees. We're going on to the jail!' And everybody in the front rows – they had been praying now for about five minutes – got up and started walking right toward the barricades and the amassed police. Stunned at first, Bull Connor yelled, 'Stop' em, stop'em!' But none of the police moved a muscle. I've never seen anything like it before or since: they all just stood watching us as if they were transfixed. Even the police dogs that had been growling and straining at their leashes when we first marched up were now perfectly calm ... We were walking right past them and Bull Connor was yelling, 'Turn on the hoses, turn on the hoses!' But the firemen didn't move either. I saw one fireman, tears in his eyes, just let the hose drop at his feet. Our people marched right between the red trucks, singing, 'I want Jesus to walk with me.' They were not rushing; it was a very slow, march ... I'll never forget one old woman who became ecstatic when she marched through the barricades. As she passed through, she shouted, 'Great God Almighty done parted the Red Sea one mo' time.'"[34]

King would later refer to what happened in Birmingham as a "majestic struggle," observing, "Bull Connor didn't know history. He knew a kind of physics that somehow didn't relate to the transphysics that we knew about." The Birmingham campaign ended victoriously in the spring of 1963, and on August 28, 1963, the great March on Washington took place and from that day onward the world will never forget King's "I Have a Dream" speech. I wish I could tell you that the events in Birmingham ended happily ever after, but I am unable to do so, because in September 1963, racists bombed the Sixteenth Street Baptist Church, where many of the rallies had been held, and four little girls in a Sunday school class became the movement's youngest martyrs. Even President Kennedy fell to an assassin's bullet in November of that year. Many more deaths occurred in the years ahead, including King's.

[34] Andrew Young, *An Easy Burden* (Waco, TX: Baylor University Press, 2008), 222-23.

The history of the African-American freedom struggle is filled with triumphs and tragedies. For some, despair and cynicism became overwhelming. The Reverend Daniel Coker in the early nineteenth century and Bishop Henry McNeal Turner in the late nineteenth century, both leading figures in the African Methodist Episcopal church, typify the many persons who gave up on America and sought a homeland in Africa. Malcolm X, a contemporary of the civil rights movement, represented those who gave up on Christianity. The riots of the mid-to-late 1960s and the ascendance of Black Nationalist organizations speak to enormous discontent. And yet time has proven, indeed the passing decades have shown, the wisdom of the great African-American theologian Howard Thurman who described an optimism that continued to grow out of troubles and difficulties. He stated it this way: "It is an optimism that uses the pessimism of life as raw material out of which it creates its own strength."[35] The biblical witness of the African-American freedom struggle reflects such strength over many generations.

The abolitionist movement and the civil rights movement hold profound lessons for the study of American democracy. They teach us about keeping faith in a country with a history that is both illustrious and flawed. Ever conscious of this duality, black Americans kept their eyes on the prize of the high calling of America, because of its revolutionary founding in the past, because of its progress in the present, and because of what it shall become someday.

[35] Howard Thurman, *Deep River and the Negro Spiritual Speaks of Life and Death* (Richmond, IN: Friends United Press, 1975), 60.

James W. C. Pennington and the Origins of African-American Religious History

By Laurie F. Maffly-Kipp

I am gratified to receive an award that bears the name of a man I have come to know very well over the last twenty years, James William Charles Pennington. You have heard the outlines of his life story, at least the part that involves Heidelberg and the Peace Movement. James Pennington was a minister and an activist. He was also, just as importantly, an intellectual. In 1841 he published one of the first comprehensive histories of African Americans, part of a genre I will refer to as "negro race histories."[1] Pennington's *A Text-book of the Origin and History of Colored People* (1841) traced the lineage of African-descended peoples from Adam in the Book of Genesis to the latest (nineteenth-century) scientific theories of racial difference. Drawing generously on the work of the Abbé Henri Grégoire, the French Roman Catholic priest, revolutionary, and antislavery advocate, Pennington argued for the equality of all human beings and the need for the immediate abolition of slavery.

Pennington, though, is much better known for his autobiographical description of his escape from slavery – and this is where I would like to begin. In 1849 he published his memoir, *The Fugitive Blacksmith*, a full eight years after the appearance of his race history. It contained the account of his daring flight from a small Maryland tobacco farm, and the book's appearance catapulted Pennington to fame as one of the foremost antislavery activists of his day.[2] His

[1] For more on the genre, see Laurie F. Maffly-Kipp, *Setting Down the Sacred Past: African American Race Histories, 1780-1920* (Cambridge, MA: Harvard University Press, 2010), ch. 5.

[2] James W. C. Pennington, *The Fugitive Blacksmith; or, Events in the History of James W. C. Pennington, Pastor of a Presbyterian Church, New York,*

renown rivaled that of his good friend, Frederick Douglass (whose marriage ceremony Pennington had performed) as well as of other "self-made" ex-slaves who lobbied for the full rights of the Negro.

In Pennington's autobiography, we hear that the eighteen-year-old slave, then named James Pembroke, set out from his home on a Sunday evening in November of 1827. Within a few days, fatigued by a lack of food and sleep, he was accosted by slave catchers who suspected he was running away. His description of that dramatic scene pivots on the question they ask him: "Who do you belong to?" He hesitated. It was a logical question coming from men who hoped to receive the bounty for any escaped slaves they managed to round up. Pennington describes his thinking as he deliberated about how to respond, and his thought process is telling: "The facts here demanded were in my breast. I knew according to the law of slavery, who I belonged to and where I came from, and I must now do one of three things – I must refuse to speak at all, or I must communicate the fact, or I must tell an untruth." Ultimately, he decided not to tell them, and he explains the logic of his decision: "the facts in this case are my private property. These men have no more right to them than a highway robber has to my purse."[3]

"Who do you belong to?" Pennington's answer to that question can be read, in the simplest terms, as a pragmatic way to maintain his freedom in a difficult situation (and surely it was). It would have been folly to give these men the name of his owner, although he risks death if his lie is discovered. And the most straightforward way to interpret his answer is that his secrecy preserves the power of his free will over the situation: He belongs only to himself – and he will never again be made the property of another human being. Slave narratives like Pennington's are the most well-known literature written by nineteenth-century African Americans, and typically they are interpreted as the most characteristic race literature, because they take us to the crux of the slave experience. Scholars have described them as stereotypically American coming-of-age stories, inasmuch as they describe the self-making of the black free man from the raw elements of enslavement. In this rendering, the

Formerly a Slave in the State of Maryland, United States, 2nd ed. (London: Charles Gilpin, 5, Bishopsgate Without, 1849).

[3] Ibid., 22.

African-American passage to freedom is a transition from servile obeisance to self-governing independence. There is no denying the narrative attraction of the story: against all odds, an intelligent and resourceful young man is able to outwit slave owners, slave catchers, and the power of Southern slave society itself and assert his dignity and individuality as he makes a new start in a free world. This is the American story, the slave's version of Horatio Alger and the self-made man. In this reading, the simple answer to "Who do you belong to?" is "myself, and no one else."

But I believe that Pennington's answer to the question "Who do you belong to?" and his association of the divulging of his identity with a theft, points us beyond the cult of American individualism to a broader understanding of the world, one that connects him to family, to nation, to a religious community, and ultimately, the international peace movement. Rather than an assertion of independence and individual free will, Pennington's response reflects the opposite: a desire to hold on to alternative forms of belonging, obligation, and allegiance. Pennington is not announcing his freedom from all constraints, but is instead mapping a new world of interconnection. In this way, he was part of an African-American intellectual tradition that can be traced back through his life and the lives of others, which sought not unfettered independence but a radically enlarged form of interdependence, one that could displace the fraught and cramped environment of white/black relationships in the U.S. with more expansive kinds of responsibilities. Those new communal ties, he suggests, constitute freedom on different terms.

Let us now step through some of Pennington's answers to that question – "Who do you belong to?" – because his self-understanding helps us to see the linkages for African Americans of his day among self, nation, religion, and the other voluntarily chosen ties that bound him and others like him. The four main affiliations to consider here are family, race, religious community, and transnational relationships. It is through Pennington's understanding of that web of interconnection that we see the significance of the "negro race history" as a statement of collective engagement and as a long answer to the question: "Who do you belong to?"

The primary affiliation for Pennington was his family, and it is possible to read his autobiography not as a narrative of self-fashioning, but instead as an explanation and apology for leaving his parents and his eleven siblings in his own flight for freedom. The intact biological family was a rare commodity in the antebellum South, since family members could be bought and sold at the will and whim of the master. Throughout Pennington's memoir he focuses on the significance of his family in shaping his worldview. He explains that he did not flee captivity sooner because he did not want to leave them behind, and he felt that it was a betrayal to do so. Unlike many enslaved African Americans, Pennington lived on a small farm with his entire extended kin, and their presence was integral to his ability to survive the moral and physical violence of the slave system. Shortly before Pennington escapes, his father is flogged by his master, and the author relates that the family thereafter "talked of it in our nightly gatherings." Pennington apparently perceived the flogging as something inflicted on all of them, a "family disgrace," and he relates that the master then began to threaten other family members "with a view to crush the spirit of the whole family." It was this event that proved the turning point in his thinking, he writes, for "in my mind and spirit, I never was a Slave after it."[4] Only through the collective familial shame experienced through his father's abuse does Pennington gain a new perspective on his condition, affording him a psychic freedom that he could not have seen on his own: his family mirrored for him a different reality. But this, of course, is the poignancy of his situation: his family connections both give him a sense of himself and they place in him the desire to flee. Yet but in so doing, he must leave behind the very thing that has sparked that initial awareness of his capability.[5]

Not surprisingly, then, it is another collective slight that forces his departure. His mother was threatened with flogging, and Pennington decides he must go. Yet this realization, forged through his ties to family, also forces a rupture with his kin and even, he feels, an abandonment of them. Pennington realizes that his departure will likely mean a permanent separation:

[4] Ibid., 7, 9.

[5] I am greatly indebted for these insights about Pennington's familial relations to William L. Andrews and his forthcoming work on family and class in African-American slave communities, especially "Family and Class in *The Fugitive Blacksmith* and *Incidents in the Life of a Slave Girl*," manuscript in author's possession.

> When I looked at my numerous family – a beloved father and mother, eleven brothers and sisters, &c.; but when I looked at slavery as such; when I looked at it in its mildest form, with all its annoyances; and above all, when I remembered that one of the chief annoyances of slavery, in the most mild form, is the liability of being at any moment sold into the worst form; it seemed that no consideration, not even that of life itself, could tempt me to give up the thought of flight.

Worse yet, he fears that his own departure might mean further punishment inflicted on his family, a knowledge that continues to haunt him.[6]

Pennington closes his memoir with a letter to his family members. They are still enslaved seventeen years after his escape, but the family is no longer intact: he has learned that some have been sold away, perhaps because of his disobedience, although he cannot know that with any certainty. His letter contains both an apology and an invitation. "If the course I took in leaving a condition which had become intolerable to me, has been made the occasion of making that condition worse to you in any way," he writes, "I do most heartily regret such a change for the worse on your part." He then urges his family to embrace the Christian faith – and couches his request both as a means for the family to once again be united and as a perspective that will place their enslavement in a different light: "We have the glorious and total weight of God's moral character in our side of the scale," he urges.

> The gospel rightly understood, taught, received, felt and practised, is anti-slavery as it is anti-sin. Just so far and so fast as the true spirit of the gospel obtains in the land, and especially in the lives of the oppressed, will the spirit of slavery sicken and become powerless like the serpent with his head pressed beneath the fresh leaves of the prickly ash of the forest.[7]

Pennington sees the acceptance of Christian faith as a way to reunite once again with his family, as well as a means to assuage their sufferings.

Pennington's family relationships thus frame his memoir just as they define and frame his self-understanding. He comes to an understanding of himself only through the collective lens of his par-

[6] Andrews, "Family and Class," 4; Pennington, *Fugitive Blacksmith*, 14.

[7] Pennington, *Fugitive Blacksmith*, 75, 76.

ents and siblings; paradoxically, it is the family lens that then compels him to escape. But he does not escape the wider perspective that was first opened to him in the family circle. Instead, he spends much of his life trying to offer a similar vantage to his enslaved kin.

This background helps us understand the goal of Pennington's *Negro Race History*, the first book he published in 1841.[8] In that text, the ex-slave used historical narrative to situate himself in broader contexts that had, quite literally, enlarged his world – and he hoped to bring that widened perspective to other African Americans as well, just as he would later try to offer some of it to his family members. This seems to me the only way to understand why his first publication after escaping enslavement, at a time when political agitation for abolition was uppermost in his mind and his work, would be an expansive world history. Why revisit Adam and Eve, or discuss the ancient Midionites, when immediate and pressing matters of basic human rights urged themselves upon the young minister from all directions? How did a return to classical civilizations further the causes for which Pennington and other African Americans so consistently fought? The answer lies in the broadening of the intellectual horizons enabled by the creation of communities of affiliation – beginning with the family, but then extending to affinities of color and circumstance (or race), of religious belief, and finally, of universal human rights.

Pennington opens his textbook with a question that will anticipate his later memoir. He begins: "In order to have my readers start with me, I must start with the question, who and whence are the colored people."[9] His book, then, serves as an extended explanation of the question asked by his potential captors and the question that defined fundamentally the system of enslavement through property rights: "Who do you belong to?" And his answer has several overlapping parts, like concentric circles that mold time and space in new ways, related to race, to religious community, and to international affiliations.

Pennington's work focuses most extensively on Africans as a people united by a common history and fate, in other words, by

[8] James W.C. Pennington, *A Textbook History of the Origin and History of the Colored People* (Hartford, CT: L. Skinner, 1841).

[9] Pennington, *Textbook*, 5.

their race (at least, in the somewhat fuzzy way that race was defined in the mid-nineteenth century). It is his realization of their common plight that helps him recognize the collective power and possibility of racial identity. He had first learned of African history through William Wright, the Quaker who had shielded him during his journey northward to freedom. His protector had taught Pennington the alphabet and some basic math, and in those lessons he learned about notable blacks such as Benjamin Banneker and Phillis Wheatley. Later, Pennington reflected on the plight of enslaved Africans as a group, and connected that community to his family relationships for the first time:

> In the spring of 1829, I found my mind unusually perplexed about the state of the slave ... I began to contrast my condition with that of ten brothers and sisters I had left in slavery, and the condition of children I saw sitting around me on the Sabbath, with their pious teachers, with that of 700,000, now 800,440 slave children ... The theme was more powerful than any my mind had ever encountered before ... The question was, what can I do for that vast body of suffering brotherhood I have left behind. To add to the weight and magnitude of the theme, I learnt for the first time how many slaves there were. The question completely staggered my mind; and finding myself more and more borne down with it, until I was in an agony."[10]

Once Pennington makes the connection between his own family members and other enslaved Africans, he finds a way of understanding his own situation and plots out his future path. His collective vision has enlarged from his family to the concept of a race in need of rescue.

In Pennington's textbook, then, he tries to spell out for other African Americans the community he sees. Like many historians of his day, the young minister drew on biblical and classical texts for his work, notably those of Josephus and Herodotus. He began his account with Adam and Eve, and traced the descent of African peoples through biblical lineage to Egypt and Ethiopia. His point was to prove the worth and dignity of Africans and their readiness for freedom, despite the claims by slave owners that the African was an inherently inferior type of being. Pennington argues against this by invoking examples of Africans who had studied in Europe and

[10] Pennington, *Fugitive Blacksmith*, 51-52.

acquitted themselves in the arts, mathematics, and languages there. He explains that ancient African civilizations had been toppled by their own vices, including a commitment to bad religion (polytheism). Despite their current state, which he found wanting, the fact of their original accomplishments and common biblical descent served as proof of African potential.

It is fascinating to see the ways that Pennington drew on the same stable of European and American intellectuals who had formed the basis for other nationalist ideologies of the day. In this way he made use of but also critiqued U.S. nationalism for its hypocrisy, anticipating the sentiments of his colleague, Frederick Douglass. On July 5, 1852, Douglass was invited to deliver a speech at an event in Rochester, New York commemorating the signing of the Declaration of Independence. By then a best-selling author and sought-after lecturer, Douglass took to the podium and paid homage to the bravery of the Revolutionary soldiers who had fought for freedom. He lauded the "great deeds" of the "truly great men" who had contended for the principle of freedom and crafted a document that would hold together a newly established nation. They loved their country, they staked their lives, and they put aside personal interest. All of this he gave its due. And then Douglass turned to what he termed the "scorching irony" of his invitation to speak that day: "What, to the American slave, is your 4th of July?" he asked. It is "*yours*, not *mine*. *You* may rejoice, I must mourn." And he then spoke of the battle being fought on a daily basis by his fellow African Americans: "Had I the ability, and could I reach the nation's ear, I would, to-day, pour out a fiery stream of biting ridicule, blasting reproach, withering sarcasm, and stern rebuke. For it is not light that is needed, but fire; it is not the gentle shower, but thunder. We need the storm, the whirlwind, and the earthquake."[11] Douglass called for war – or, more accurately, he called for a just conclusion to the war that had begun in 1776 and had never been completed. The ex-fugitive slave evoked an alternative rendering of history that threatened to completely upend the proscribed rituals of celebration and the paeans to American liberty expected on that occasion.

[11] Frederick Douglass, *Oration, Delivered in Corinthian Hall, Rochester, July 5th, 1852* (Rochester: Lee, Mann & Co., 1852), 15, 20.

Pennington's text broached racial identity with even broader brush strokes, since he traced the community from the beginning of sacred history to the present. It is that long perspective that allows for a different interpretation of slavery: not as an individual cause fought between master and slave, but as a collective struggle that had begun centuries earlier. "Let this point then, stand in bold relief to the view of the world. And let it be fairly understood that the American slave-holder and his apologists are patrons of Rome and the dark age!" Pennington announced. Seen as part of a longer span, slavery is not the result of personal failings but a systemic injustice visited on Africans not just now, but on many others in times past. While this might seem small comfort to the slave, it was a popular tactic of historical explanation in the nineteenth century. Situating African enslavement as part of the rise and inevitable fall of civilizations established African Americans as part of a nation alongside other glorious powers – one subject to the same laws of nature, yes, but also one that could provide an enduring source of sustenance in the face of oppression. As he later wrote, "Adversity, to the race, has been a training school. And not only has the race come to exercise a higher range of thought and a deeper reflection in regard to its own relative position, among other races of the world; but a more extended view is taken of all the localities of the race."[12]

Pennington's religious faith, alongside family and racial ties, also played a central role in his web of connections. Recall that his first impulse in reuniting with his family through his letter from the autobiography is to convert them to Christianity. For Pennington, churches were both an efficient way to organize for political action and a form of collective obligation that, like families and nations, gained him greater distance from the aggressive pull of the master-slave relationship.

Upon his arrival in the north in the late 1820s, Pennington immediately found himself at home in a free black community anchored in the church. Antebellum African-American Protestants created and sustained a religious community anchored by reform and activism, Bible study, and a devotion to theological interpretations of divine justice. Religion not only provided meaning and sol-

[12] Pennington, *Textbook*, 44; Pennington, "The Self-Redeeming Power of the Colored Races of the World," *Anglo-African Magazine*, I (1859), 314-15.

ace, but it fueled passion and inspired coordinated action. Having changed his name to James W.C. Pennington to avoid detection, since he was still an escaped slave, Pennington arrived in New York, where he converted to Christianity and taught himself Greek and Hebrew; he then applied and was accepted as the first black student at Yale University. The only proviso was that he had to sit in the back of the room and not speak. He was thus an eavesdropper on a Reformed religious tradition that captivated and transformed his life and which he then used as a resource to reorient the meaning of the violence done on a daily basis to African Americans.[13]

Pennington's religious belief helped him to interpret the war against slavery not just as a fight among nations, but also as an ongoing battle against sin. In the 1840s and 1850s, as pastor of Congregational and later Presbyterian Churches in New York, Hartford, and Portland (Maine), he fleshed out the contours of this struggle. Three themes characterized Pennington's accounts: first, the war had been fought – bodily and materially, not just psychologically or as a metaphor for a loosely-defined struggle – for decades if not centuries; second, the war was a sacred cause that could not be disentangled from God's plan for the redemption of humanity as a whole; third, the war was international, involving enslavement in nations beyond U.S. borders. In his speeches, and in his *Text Book,* Pennington argued that the struggle over slavery must be understood as part of a longer and larger piece of God's providential plan.

In an 1856 speech in Hartford, Pennington adopted military rhetoric in his description of the Christian abolitionist effort: he noted that early abolitionists "prepared themselves, step by step, to attack slavery in the colonies. For forty-three years they battled slavery in the metropolis; thirty-five years they wrestled with the slave-trade, and thirty-one years conflict had they with slavery in the colonies."[14] Pennington and others quite self-consciously used the language of war to describe events throughout this period, including the slave uprisings of Denmark Vesey, Nat Turner and John

[13] The best full-length treatment of Pennington is Herman E. Thomas, *James W.C. Pennington: African American Churchman and Abolitionist* (New York: Garland Publishing, 1995). On his time at Yale, see p. 77 ff.

[14] Pennington, "An Address, delivered at Hartford, Conn., on the First of August, 1856" (Hartford, CT: Case, Tiffany, and Company, 1856), 8.

Brown, as an attempt to shift the rhetoric from the accommodation or gradualism favored by more moderate anti-slavery activists to that of active Christian warfare. In outlining the incidents of violence both large and small conducted daily against African Americans, Pennington seemed to press the questions: what does it take to call this war? How much more blood needs to be shed? Did only the blood of white men count as an indicator of legitimate war?

Biblical imagery proved critical in shifting the terms in ways that included African Americans as part of the body politic – and as agents in the war rather than merely its precipitating cause. In an 1843 speech protesting the relaxation of Indian emigration policies, Pennington evoked the Pauline metaphor of the body:

> The human family, taken as a whole, are like the body. Each class is a limb; every limb sustains it appropriate relation. Strike off a limb, and you injure the whole body. To treat any one class of the human family without a respect to the relationship they sustain, is to do injury to the entire body, and to diffuse pain throughout it. Here is the exact position of that limb of the human family which I represent today. For hundreds of years it has been dismembered from the trunk, and hence mutual pain, mutual disease, mutual agony, mutual trouble throughout the whole body.[15]

Positing African Americans as legitimate actors in American society would, black leaders felt, force whites to see that the war was already ongoing, and that it was linked directly to the failings of white-led nations. Some, like the black Episcopal minister James Holly, proposed that the best solution would be to establish an equally strong Negro nationality that could serve as an effective counter-force to the willfulness of Europe and the U.S. Pennington and most other Protestant leaders located the problem in a deeper recognition of human sinfulness – to which all human beings, black or white, were subject. The answer, then, was not to fight might with might, but to convert the world to Christ. Pennington traced these conflicts back to Adam and Eve, framing the problem of slavery as part of the flaw of original sin. In this sense, no model better served black leaders than that of original sin itself; slavery, as a sign and

15 Pennington, Article from *The Anti-Slavery Reporter*, June 28, 1843, in the *Black Abolitionist Archive*, http://research.udmercy.edu/digital_collections/baa/Pennington_06951spe.pdf, accessed June 4, 2014.

symbol of that sin, infected everything and everyone, and could only be eradicated once and for all by a radical and divinely-ordained overturning of the social order. In the meantime, Christian action could mitigate its most serious effects. Pennington's objective was to map the contours of this sacred history and to connect the dots of African oppression at the hands of Europeans and Euro-Americans in order to right the moral compass. Historiography, therefore, was intrinsically linked to divine redemption and to African freedom.

Scholars of American history have long looked to Abraham Lincoln's eloquent theological interpretation of the Civil War as one of the most complex statements of its significance. No doubt, African Americans loved Lincoln for the freedoms he enabled on their behalf. Sometime shortly after the president delivered his Second Inaugural Address, Frederick Douglass apparently said to him, "Mr. Lincoln, that was a sacred effort," one that sounded "more like a sermon than a state paper." Douglass recognized Lincoln's rhetoric because he had heard it in black churches for decades previously and had certainly learned about it through the writings of his friend James Pennington. Throughout the 1840s and 1850s, Pennington and other black Protestant leaders used their own theology of history to explicate the religious meaning of the war, and they did so in a way that moved well beyond the binary and national terms expressed by the President. Theirs was a complex and sometimes contradictory understanding of sacred history that they felt would better illuminate the full measure of the American problem – not simply a problem of slavery, but of the failure of whites to recognize the fellow Christians in their midst. "When you have made of man a slave by a seven-fold process of selling, bartering and chaining, and garnished him with that rough and bloody brush, the cart-whip, and set him to the full by blowing into the eyes of his mind cloud after cloud of moral darkness," Pennington concluded, "his own immortality still remains."[16]

In his 1856 address Pennington reframed the war in terms that were arguably even more profoundly infused with biblical and national imagery. "With the Bible and the Declaration of Independence for our weapons," he proclaimed, "we will make a bold push, for the day begins. In the course of events, it dawns. The fruitful

[16] Pennington, "Address, 1856," 18.

womb of time is already pregnant with another heir, and *that* heir is ours. The last was born yonder, but the next shall be born here."[17] The dawn of Emancipation meant no less than the birth of a new savior and the dawn of a new era of sacred history – one measured not only by the actions of white brothers in arms, but by the participation of all Americans in a society of equality and freedom.

Pennington also drew attention away from the conflict as a brotherly fight among states by framing it as part of an international movement. This is a point that is too often ignored: even as Northern and Southern whites remained focused on conflict as a problem of nation-building, African Americans consistently drew attention to the broader scope of the war. Pennington noted that the Indian indenture system in the 1840s amounted to a "new form of slave-trading." In 1859 his Episcopal colleague James Holly protested the artificial separation of the problem of slavery in the U.S. from what he termed the "piratical depradations [sic] carried on against the African race" throughout the world. "The deepest and most radical cause of slavery is not to be sought for in this country," Holly insisted, but in the voracious appetites of modern nation-states for resources and labor. To solve the problem of slavery in the U.S. alone, they insisted, would not end the war.[18]

This is the framing of the story, then, that brings us to Heidelberg in 1849. Pennington's intellectual and physical journey to that place was many years in the making. Through his focus on family, on race and nation, and on Christian faith, he had sought consistently to introduce other African Americans, as well as whites, to a historical consciousness that could make sense of the evils of African slavery and that might also precipitate its eradication. He later wrote, "A man who cannot at the glance of thought traverse the map of the world is mentally incapable of appreciating civilization in its extended sense."[19] Like many other African Americans, including William Wells Brown and Frederick Douglass, Pennington looked to Europe in particular as a beacon of hope, both for the practical help it could offer as a shelter and logistical supporter

[17] Ibid., 19-20.

[18] James Theodore Holly, "Thoughts on Hayti, no. VI," *Anglo-African Magazine*, I (1859), 364.

[19] Pennington, "Self-Redeeming Power," 315.

for anti-slavery, but also as a reminder of the commitment to universal human rights held out so tantalizingly by the promises of the American Revolution but withheld from African Americans. During a previous trip to England, Pennington was hailed as an accomplished preacher and, according to one of his contemporaries, "moved on a footing of social and intellectual equality with the ministers and people of his own persuasion."[20] By that the author meant not other African Americans or other ex-slaves, but other independent Protestants. In this environment, Pennington could once again reinvent himself outside the bounds of slavery. In his British speaking tours, Frederick Douglass likewise loved to take jabs at American hypocrisy regarding African Americans. As he wrote to one of his abolitionist colleagues, "I have crossed three thousand miles of the perilous deep. Instead of a democratic government, I am under a monarchical government . . . I breathe, and lo! the chattel becomes a man."[21]

Ironically, once Pennington had published his autobiography, in which he documented that personal journey taken many years before, he recognized the dangers of staying in the United States. He was, after all, still technically a slave. He knew that once his identity was revealed, he would be prey for anyone wishing to collect a reward for his capture. For those reasons, he left the United States for Europe. There, still a fugitive from the Slave Power, Pennington delivered a stirring speech to the assembly at the Second General Peace Congress in Paris in August 1849. He spoke of slavery and of his hope for the eradication of the institution based on principles of Christian faith and international cooperation. He closed with the following invitation: "We invite the great nations of the earth to come under the influence of this principle. Cherish goodwill to their enemies, keep the peace of the world's community; and, so far from ever hearing the roar of the cannon again, we shall soon hear that the kingdoms of this

[20] Armistead Wilson, *A Tribute for the Negro: Being a Vindication of the Moral, Intellectual, and Religious Capabilities of the Coloured Portion of Mankind; with Particular Reference to the African Race* (Manchester, England: William Irwin, 1848), 408.

[21] Benjamin Soskis, "Heroic Exile: The Transatlantic Development of Frederick Douglass, 1845-1847," Online at the Gilder Lehrman Center, http://www.yale.edu/glc/soskis/fr-1.htm, accessed June 4, 2014.

world are become the kingdoms of our God, and of his Christ. If the gospel be true, our course is right, and must prevail."[22]

It was during that trip that he also met with Friedrich Wilhelm Carové, a Catholic and philosopher residing in Heidelberg who was an ardent proponent of religious toleration. We do not know with certainty whether Pennington suggested the bestowal of a doctorate or the idea came from Carové. Clearly, both saw the significance of that possibility, and Carové advocated on behalf of his friend. Both, indeed, understood the award as a signal of something much larger than Pennington's individual attainments. For Carové, the award marked a partial collective atonement for the atrocities of the slave trade; for Pennington, it measured the capabilities of all people of color who had been enslaved. Yet it would be misleading to see this merely as a strategic ploy to expiate guilt or publicize a cause. Pennington's race history and subsequent writings – indeed, his whole career – focused on building and recognizing human connections across worlds of difference based on race, national identity, and religion. Fostered in the early years of his family relationships, Pennington's desire for mutual obligation and understanding began with his flight for freedom. Rather than seeing that journey as an effort to avoid revealing his own identity to potential captors, or an individualized road to an unfettered self, we must recognize the deep desires for connection exemplified in Pennington's work and articulated most clearly in his race history.

Pennington also never stopped trying to free his immediate family. Their situation remained precarious and tied to his own fate by the continuing resentment of their master. Throughout the 1840s he made attempts to purchase their titles, but was rebuffed by his former owner. Eventually, he raised enough funds to free two of his brothers and his father, who fled to Canada. His mother, who had been sold further south, was also eventually found and freed, as were several of his sisters. Pennington raised enough money to purchase his own freedom in 1851. Yet even legal titles could not protect family members from danger, since slave catchers ran a lucrative business in rounding up free blacks and selling them south on

[22] *Report of the Proceedings of the Second General Peace Congress, held in Paris, on the 22nd, 23rd, and 24th of August, 1849* (London: Charles Gilpin, 1850), 85.

the black market. In 1854, Pennington's brother Stephen and two of his nephews were arrested in New York City and sold south, and the minister raised another large sum of money to get them returned.

It is little wonder, then, that James W. C. Pennington devoted his writing to fashioning communities that he felt would be impervious to catastrophic loss. Families were precarious and easily injured, but races, religions, and international coalitions had endured and would continue. The promises of ancient Africa, of Christian universalism, and yes, of a community of scholars from Heidelberg, enabled the fulfillment of that promise.

James W. C. Pennington and Mark Twain: Slavery and the Moral Conscience of American Literature

By William L. Andrews

More than any other literary form in United States' history, the African-American slave narrative dramatized how profoundly chattel slavery undermined and perverted the defining institutions of the American republic, thereby corrupting and threatening the social, economic, religious, and political character of the United Sates. Chattel slavery, we should remember, was one of the five fundamental institutions that governed the identity and destiny of the United States. The other four institutions defined the social, economic, religious, and political character of the nation. In the political sphere, the defining institution of the United States was and is representative democracy. In the religious sphere, the defining institution was Protestant Christianity. In the economic sphere, the institution of capitalism fueled the rise of the new country to superpower status. Finally, the defining social institution of the United States has been for generations marriage and the family. One could argue that public education has also been a tremendously important social institution in the United States, but the idea of education at public expense for the masses of Americans was not a priority for the founders of the nation and did not become widespread until after the Civil War.

Representative democracy in politics, capitalism in economics, Protestant Christianity in religious life, and marriage and family in social life constitute four of the five defining institutions of the United States from the early Republic through the nineteenth century. Chattel slavery became the fifth defining institution of the United States because it perverted and threatened the very existence of all four of the other founding institutions. Slavery made a mockery of marriage, not to mention the family, especially for African Americans, by refusing to recognize the inviolability of slave marriages or the families that resulted from them. Husbands and wives were routinely sold away from each other, and children were routinely parted from their parents through sale when deemed necessary or profitable by the slaveholders. Slavery certainly undermined the very idea of a free market economy in half of the United States until 1865. Although many slaves participated to a limited extent in market activities in some parts of the antebellum South, unfree and uncompensated workers could not, by definition, be free economic agents or make choices, rational or otherwise, about how they would dispose of their labor. As for political liberty, slavery denied the right to vote to millions of persons while the notorious Three-Fifths compromise, which recognized the enslaved population of the South only insofar as it would increase the political clout of the white South in the U.S. Congress, grotesquely distorted representative democracy in the country as a whole. The backwash of slavery – segregation and racial discrimination – continues to hamper democracy in the United States in the twenty-first century. In the religious realm, slavery distorted or denied Protestant Christianity's fundamental tenet, namely, the priesthood of all believers, by restricting freedom of worship and access to the Bible for the large majority of slaves. The illiteracy enforced by slavery on the large majority of its victims was partly designed to prevent slaves from reading the Bible. Thus, slavery demanded that black people accept the idea that their spiritual inferiority to whites was one more reason for their divinely-appointed social, economic, and moral subordination to their enslavers.

Antebellum slave narrators addressed their white readers as tribunes of a largely voiceless people whose exploitation was, to many whites in the North as well as the South, simply a given, not a moral, social, political, or religious issue at all. After the Civil War, as white Americans wanted increasingly to forget about slavery while celebrating the reunification of the nation, former slaves continued to write narratives about their enslavement, if only to create a lasting record of their experience under America's "peculiar institution." Morphing into what we call today the "neo-slave narrative," the nineteenth-century slave narrative tradition evolved into novels, one of which I'll discuss in this essay, that reinterpreted slavery and its heritage for successive generations. The slave narrative had a profound effect on the most widely-read white American novel of the entire nineteenth century, namely Harriet Beecher Stowe's *Uncle Tom's Cabin* (1852). In the twentieth and early twenty-first centuries, the slave narrative has had widespread influence on American fiction, as the following major American novels attest: Ralph Ellison's *Invisible Man* (1952), Margaret Walker's *Jubilee* (1965), Ernest Gaines's *The Autobiography of Miss Jane Pittman* (1971), Alex Haley's *Roots* (1976), Octavia Butler's *Kindred* (1979), Sherley Ann Williams's *Dessa Rose* (1986), and Charles Johnson's *Middle Passage* (1990). Over the last fifty years, three Pulitzer Prize winning novels have kept the slave narrative tradition very much alive and timely: William Styron's *The Confessions of Nat Turner* (1967), Toni Morrison's *Beloved* (1987), and *The Known World* (2003) by Edward P. Jones. We can also follow the formal and thematic tracks of the slave narrative in key twentieth-century African-American autobiographies, such as Booker T. Washington's *Up From Slavery* (1901), Richard Wright's *Black Boy (American Hunger)* (1991), and *The Autobiography of Malcolm X* (1965). The slave narrative tradition lives on in the 2014 Golden Globe and Oscar-winning movie, *12 Years a Slave.*

In this essay I begin by noting the influence of James W. C. Pennington's fugitive slave narrative on Mark Twain's contribution to the American slave narrative tradition, *Adventures of Huckleberry Finn* (1884). I then discuss this classic American novel as a post-Civil War fictional narrative of American slavery. My ultimate aim is to explore the strengths and limitations, from the standpoint of racial portraiture, of perhaps the most famous novel in American history.

In the summer of 1849, four years after the landmark appearance of the *Narrative of the Life of Frederick Douglass, An American Slave*, a London publisher brought out a short autobiography entitled *The Fugitive Blacksmith; or, Events in the History of James W. C. Pennington, Pastor of a Presbyterian Church, New York, Formerly a Slave in the State of Maryland, United States.*[1] A year and two subsequent editions later, the Rev. Pennington wrote his publisher to say how pleased he was with "the rapid sale of the Sixth Thousand

[1] James W. C. Pennington, *The Fugitive Blacksmith* (London: Charles Gilpin, 1849). Unless otherwise noted, all quotations will be from this edition.

of *The Fugitive Blacksmith*," a pace of sales that any author in mid-nineteenth-century America would have been very pleased with.[2] Twice as many readers bought *The Fugitive Blacksmith* in two years as bought *Moby Dick* in 40 years, that is, from 1851, when Herman Melville's book was published, to 1891, when Melville died.[3] One of the reasons for the popularity of *The Fugitive Blacksmith* stemmed from its suspenseful account of the author's 1827 escape to Philadelphia from a plantation eighty miles south of Baltimore. On the third day of his flight to freedom, the fugitive, whose slave name was Jim Pembroke, was captured just a few miles from his home by a group of suspicious Maryland farmers. When he could produce no free papers attesting to his right to be on a northbound road alone, Pennington was taken to a tavern for questioning.

> "'Who do you belong to, and where did you come from?'" the white men demanded. "'If you will not put me in jail, I will now tell you where I am from,'" the overmatched fugitive promised.[4] Then, under extreme pressure and with his chance for freedom on the line, Jim Pembroke spun out this wholly spontaneous and completely false tale. "'A few weeks ago, I was sold from the eastern shore to a slave-trader, who had a large gang, and set out for Georgia, but when he got to a town in Virginia, he was taken sick, and died with the small-pox. Several of his gang also died with it, so that the people in the town became alarmed, and did not wish the gang to remain among them. No one claimed us, or wished to have anything to do with us; I left the rest, and thought I would go somewhere and get work.'"[5]

The response to this wonderful lie was immediate. "I perceived that a panic began to seize some, at the idea that I was one of a small-pox gang. Several who had clustered near me, moved off to a respectful distance. One or two left the bar-room, and murmured, 'better let the small-pox nigger go.'"[6] Much more loosely guarded after telling his ingenious lie, Pennington soon eluded his captors and made his way to freedom. In subsequent years he became an ordained min-

[2] James W.C. Pennington, *The Fugitive Blacksmith*, 3rd ed. (London: Charles Gilpin, 1850), 16.

[3] G. Thomas Tanselle, "The Sales of Melville's Books," *Harvard Library Bulletin* 18 (April 1969): 195-215.

[4] Pennington, *The Fugitive Blacksmith*, 24.

[5] Ibid., 24.

[6] Ibid., 24-5.

ister, a leading civil rights activist, and an African-American hero of such national prominence that Harriet Beecher Stowe's *Uncle Tom's Cabin* singled out Pennington by name, along with Frederick Douglass, as black men who had elevated themselves from slavery "to highly respectable stations in society."[7]

Thirty-five years after *The Fugitive Blacksmith*, one of the most famous episodes in *Huckleberry Finn* regaled its readers as Huck outwits a pair of slavecatchers intent on searching his raft for a runaway slave named, interestingly, Jim. Huck's talent for extemporaneous lying is never demonstrated better than when he maneuvers the slave-catchers into the conclusion that all aboard the raft are infected with, interestingly, smallpox. The aftermath of this episode shows how pivotal Huck's lie is to a struggle that defines his moral growth through the entire book. Jim admires Huck's smallpox deception, calling it "de smartes' dodge," that is, the slickest trick, the slave had ever seen put over on white men.[8] But Huck can take little satisfaction in his triumph. As Mark Twain explained to a friend, Huck's lie calls attention to the inner struggle between the boy's "sound heart" and his "deformed conscience."[9]

Huck's socially-conditioned conscience – we might call it his superego – always upbraids him for sheltering and protecting Jim in defiance of the laws of slaveholding Missouri, where Huck grew up. When Huck and Jim approach the point in the Mississippi River where Jim feels he is on the threshold of freedom, Huck's "conscience got to stirring me up hotter than ever," commanding him

[7] "In all states of the Union we see men, but yesterday burst from the shackles of slavery, who, by a self-educating force, which cannot be too much admired, have risen to highly respectable stations in society. Pennington, among clergymen, Douglas [sic] and [Samuel Ringgold] Ward, among editors, are well known instances." Harriet Beecher Stowe, *Uncle Tom's Cabin*, ed. Elizabeth Ammons (1852; New York: W. W. Norton, 1994), 388.

[8] Mark Twain [Samuel Clemens], *The Adventures of Huckleberry Finn,* eds. Sculley Bradley, Richmond Croom Beatty, E. Hudson Long, and Thomas Cooley, 2nd. ed. (1885; NY: W. W. Norton, 1977), 76. All quotations from the novel are taken from this edition, abbreviated Twain, *HF,* unless otherwise noted.

[9] Clemens referred to Huckleberry Finn as "a book of mine where a sound heart and a deformed conscience come into collision and conscience suffers defeat." Mark Twain, *Mark Twain's Letters,* 1876-1880, Volume 3: 1878, © 2001 The Mark Twain Foundation. (Berkeley: University of California Press, 2003), 427-428.

to paddle to shore and turn Jim in.[10] Only the unexpected meeting with the two slave-catchers prevents Huck from doing the bidding of his corrupted conscience. The smallpox deception represents Huck's first major internal battle with his conscience, a war that reaches its climax after Jim has been captured and imprisoned on the farm of Silas Phelps. Huck wants to help Jim but his conscience objects with a vengeance, reminding him that "people that acts as I'd been acting about that nigger goes to everlasting fire."[11] To prove to his conscience that he has truly reformed, Huck drafts a letter informing Miss Watson, Jim's owner, as to his whereabouts so she can recapture him. The letter makes Huck feel "all washed clean of sin," but his heart reminds him of how good Jim has been to him throughout their journey down the Mississippi.[12] As a result, Huck tears up his letter. "'All right then, I'll *go* to hell,'" he says, and resolves to steal Jim away from his captors.[13]

There are obvious similarities between the smallpox lie spontaneously concocted by the fugitive Jim Pembroke when captured by threatening whites and the smallpox lie Huck Finn spontaneously invents to help protect a fugitive slave named Jim from white slave-catchers. There is an additional parallel between the 1849 slave narrative and the 1884 novel. Though successful in evading external pursuers, neither Pennington nor Huck could escape the judgments of conscience, which, in both books, assessed grave moral consequences to lying, even in order to save a fugitive slave. The Rev. James Pennington suspended his narrative to describe what he called the "GREAT MORAL DILEMMA" that beset him after he told his smallpox lie.[14] Similarly, in a chapter of his novel subtitled "A Dilemma," Mark Twain shows Huck battling with his conscience over his protection of Jim and the eternal punishment he will receive for doing such a sinful thing. In the end, the narrators of both *The Fugitive Blacksmith* and *Huckleberry Finn* achieve dignity as well as sympathy because they are willing to risk body and soul for a black man's right to freedom.

[10] Twain, *HF*, 74.
[11] Twain, *HF*, 168.
[12] Twain, *HF*, 169.
[13] Twain, *HF*, 169.
[14] Pennington, *The Fugitive Blacksmith*, 21.

Was there a point in the life of Mark Twain when he read *The Fugitive Blacksmith*? I think there was. In the summer and fall of 1853, while seventeen-year-old Sam Clemens was working in New York City as a printer, he lived approximately twelve blocks from the Shiloh Presbyterian Church, pastored by the Rev. James W.C. Pennington, a locally renowned black leader whose name had just been trumpeted to the world by none other than Harriet Beecher Stowe in her blockbuster bestseller, *Uncle Tom's Cabin*. Striking internal parallels between Pennington's narrative and Clemens's novel, together with the real possibility that young Sam Clemens could have discovered Pennington's widely-distributed narrative during the many hours he spent in a local free printer's library during his New York City stay, lead me to believe that as a young man, Sam Clemens read *The Fugitive Blacksmith*. Pennington's artful smallpox lie and the subsequent "great moral dilemma" he felt in his conscience impressed young Sam Clemens, settling somewhere in his creative unconscious to surface 35 years later in altered form in *Huckleberry Finn*.[15]

If James W.C. Pennington had lived to read *Huckleberry Finn*, he surely would have appreciated the way Mark Twain adapted the smallpox lie in *The Fugitive Blacksmith* to help a runaway named Jim stay clear of those Mississippi River slave-catchers. But the former Jim Pembroke would likely have been dismayed by the failure of Mark Twain's own conscience by the end of his celebrated novel.

Mark Twain's knowledge of and participation in the slave narrative tradition was a point of distinction for him among white American writers of the late nineteenth century. Ten years before *Huckleberry Finn*, Samuel Langhorne Clemens made an important contribution to both white American literature and the slave narrative tradition in the post-Civil War era by writing "A True Story." This was Mark Twain's first publication for the *Atlantic Monthly*, a major American magazine, whose imprimatur meant a lot to Clemens's efforts to validate himself as a literary man.[16] In "A True

[15] This research is documented in William L. Andrews, "Mark Twain and James W.C. Pennington: Huckleberry Finn's Smallpox Lie," *Studies in American Fiction* 9 (Spring 1981): 103-112.

[16] Mark Twain, [Samuel Clemens], "A True Story," *Atlantic Monthly* (November 1874): 591-594.

Story," Clemens transcribed the oral narration of "Auntie Rachel" (Mary Ann Cord) as she recalled her trials in slavery and her unexpected, heart-warming reunion with her son at the end of the Civil War. The title of "A True Story" and the note that Mark Twain used to preface it – "Repeated Word for Word as I Heard It" – call attention to the author's desire that the piece be read not as a work of fiction but as a "true" rendition of a former slave's touching and inspiring autobiography. Mark Twain had good reason to be proud of this contribution to the slave narrative tradition.

Quite obviously, Mark Twain's greatest novel incorporates the American slave narrative's central theme, a male fugitive slave's quest for freedom. However, we should not ignore some striking differences between Mark Twain's novel and previous narratives of actual fugitives from slavery. Most slave narratives picture the fugitive's escape as a time of severe trial, entailing both physical and psychological struggle and testing, as though the fugitive were undergoing a rite of passage. However, the fugitive in Mark Twain's novel undergoes very little psychological or physical struggle as he floats down the Mississippi River. The novel contains a powerful rendition of the struggles within the fugitive's companion, a white boy, who must struggle with his conscience, as already pointed out. But Mark Twain's story says almost nothing about internal struggles that affect Jim as *he* tries to escape. Instead, the novel is almost entirely focused on a white boy's mental and spiritual struggles.

Nor does Mark Twain's runaway slave meet with any physical struggles, such as Pennington faced when he was on the run in Maryland. At one point in *The Fugitive Blacksmith*, Pennington says that he was ready to use a rock as a weapon to break the kneecap of a white pursuer. By contrast, Mark Twain's fugitive slave never has a physical confrontation with anyone; his determination to be free is never tested in this fashion. By putting Huck in the role of Jim's intermediary and protector, Mark Twain ensured that Huck would have plenty of moral dilemmas and decisions while acting, again and again, as the agent of both his and Jim's freedom. At the same time, however, the decision to associate Jim's search for freedom with neither the internal nor the external kinds of struggle that beset fugitive slaves like Pennington meant that, throughout the novel, white readers see Jim as largely an observer, not an initiator of the action, a non-confrontational and increasingly passive figure as the novel progresses.

This is significant because of the way white readers of the novel responded to Jim. What impressed the popular academic critic William Lyon Phelps when he commented on Mark Twain's runaway slave was "the peculiar harmlessness of Jim," which Phelps pronounced "beautiful to contemplate" in his 1907 assessment of Clemens's literary career.[17] Professor Phelps's response echoed that of the London *Saturday Review*, which concluded that in Jim "the essential simplicity and kindliness and generosity of the Southern negro have never been better shown."[18] The fact that contemporary white reviewers of *Huckleberry Finn* were charmed by Jim's "peculiar harmlessness," his "kindliness," and his "simplicity" suggests just how successful Mark Twain was in revising the pre-Civil War image of the fugitive as a man made desperate, even dangerous, by his consuming desire for liberty at all costs.[19] Mark Twain's Jim would prove himself "simple," "kind," and above all "harmless," thereby suggesting to white readers in post-Reconstruction America that freedom could be safely conferred on this sort of black man without worrying about what he might to do with it.[20]

[17] As quoted in Louis J. Budd, ed. *Critical Essays on Mark Twain, 1867-1910* (Boston: G.K. Hall, 1982), 196.

[18] As quoted in *The Adventures of Huckleberry Finn*, 2nd ed. (New York: Norton, 1977), 294.

[19] These adjectives chosen by reviewers to describe Jim are consonant with those Clemens used in his autobiography to characterize "Uncle Dan'l," a slave owned by Clemens's uncle, who furnished a model for Jim. According to Clemens, Daniel was "a faithful and affectionate good friend, ally and adviser" to white boys, a man "whose sympathies were wide and warm, and whose heart was honest and simple and knew no guile." In several novels, "under his own name and as 'Jim,'" Mark Twain noted, he had "carted [Daniel] all around – to Hannibal, down the Mississippi on a raft, and even across the Desert of Sahara in a balloon – and he has endured it all with a patience and friendliness and loyalty which were his birthright." See Mark Twain [Samuel Clemens], *Mark Twain's Own Autobiography*, ed. Michael J. Kiskis, 2nd ed. (Madison: University of Wisconsin Press, 2010), 115.

[20] For a discussion of a parallel kind of domestication of Jim's language, so that his dialect did not communicate anything smacking of hostility to whites, see David Sewell, *Mark Twain's Languages: Discourse, Dialogue, and Linguistic Variety* (Berkeley: University of California Press, 1987), 95.

Let me emphasize here that I am not suggesting that Clemens gave his readers nothing to admire or honor in Jim. Jim is kind to Huck early in their association. Jim is also a prudent and pragmatic adviser to Huck before they meet up with the two conmen, the King and the Duke. But Mark Twain did not conceive of Jim as a latter-day Frederick Douglass or James Pennington, two black men whose narratives portray them on lonely, desperate, intrepid quests for freedom that elevate each to heroic status. Mark Twain's Jim has a down-to-earth, pragmatic reason for escaping. Hearing that his owner is thinking of selling him, Jim runs, leaving his family and the life he has known to escape being sold into the worst form of slavery imaginable, life on the cotton fields or sugar plantations of the Deep South. There is no indication in the novel that prior to hearing of his owner's plans, Jim had any intention of trying to escape. In many respects, therefore, Mark Twain's Jim seems more ordinary and representative, a more realistic African-American everyman, rather than an extraordinary, larger-than-life figure like a Douglass or a Pennington, men impelled by personal pride and a determined will to seize freedom at all costs. Jim's down-to-earth representativeness also comes across in his lack of conventional sophistication, his illiteracy, his dialect speech, his love of his own family, and his unabashed affection for Huck. Jim commands our respect for what Huck correctly recognizes as Jim's consistently good judgment – Huck calls it Jim's "uncommon level head."[21] Jim also deserves credit for his paternal concern for the fatherless white boy who, early in their journey, depends on Jim a good deal. One way we see Huck mature in wisdom is when, early in his journey downriver with Jim, Huck realizes that Jim is not a man to be trifled with or made fun of, even though back in St. Petersburg, Huck joined Tom Sawyer in tricking Jim simply for a laugh. On the river, where he is no longer willing to defer to Huck simply because he's white, Jim becomes a different, more outspoken man. Filled with a longing to gain his freedom, Jim also announces that after he gets to freedom, he plans to return to his home with some abolitionists and free his family. Hearing Jim talk so independently is what sets Huck's corrupt conscience to nagging him over helping a slave escape. But he has learned not to try to argue Jim out of his plan to steal his own family and free them.

[21] Twain, *HF*, 64.

The first one-third of *Huckleberry Finn* boldly revises key features of the nineteenth-century American novel, particularly its focus on a white American male struggling against social restraint and longing for freedom, an image retailed by such renowned white male writers as James Fenimore Cooper, Nathaniel Hawthorne, and Herman Melville. Mark Twain's novel doesn't depart from the work of his male literary predecessors when he portrays Huck on the run from female supervision in search of freedom from what Huck detests as "civilization."[22] What makes the novel remarkable is that a black man, a fugitive slave, accompanies Huck aboard the raft. Jim is in search of freedom from actual legal enslavement, a specific historical injustice. Jim's goal is not just escape, as it is for Huck, but empowerment so he can return and liberate his family. These dimensions of Jim's story, along with the mounting identification of Huck with Jim's goals, are what make Mark Twain's novel so original. Mark Twain gives us Jim, and through him Huck, confronting the enormous problem of racial slavery that had placed the nation in crisis and put the very existence of the United States in jeopardy.

A key turning point early in the novel is Huck's decision in chapter 11 to accompany Jim in the latter's quest for freedom, even though to do so, is very risky for this white boy. After learning that whites are trying to track down the runaway, Huck rouses Jim on Jackson's Island with the alarm, "hump yourself, Jim . . . They're after us."[23] Huck's words – "they after *us*" – show that the white boy has come to identify with the fugitive slave's predicament. We almost forget that, in fact, nobody is after Huck; everyone thinks he's dead. But plenty of whites want to find Jim, hoping to claim the reward that's out for his recapture. By having Huck *join* Jim in fleeing down the river, Mark Twain encouraged his readers to credit the white boy for subsuming his longing for escape under the fugitive slave's quest for freedom. In the early days of their journey together, Huck gains enough wisdom and respect for Jim that, in chapter 15, Huck feels obliged to ask the black man's pardon for the stupid jokes Huck has tried to play on Jim. Before getting on the

[22] See Nina Baym, "Melodramas of Beset Manhood: How Theories of American Fiction Exclude Women Authors," in *The New Feminist Criticism,* ed. Elaine Showalter (New York: Pantheon, 1985), 63-80.

[23] Twain, *HF*, 54.

raft with Jim, Huck could not have imagined ever voluntarily "humbling himself to a nigger," as he puts it.[24] But in the first one-third of the novel Jim becomes an imposing adult figure in Huck's estimation, so much so that Huck cannot betray him in his flight to the free states.[25] Huck's decision to protect Jim from the slave-catchers, in conscious disregard of his ingrained sense of racial superiority as well as his conscience, makes a powerful point about what is most fundamentally at issue in the first one-third of *Huckleberry Finn*. The issue is, will Jim get his freedom, to which Huck has committed himself in an unprecedented interracial partnership?

Jim's goal is getting to freedom as quickly and directly as possible. Huck, by contrast, is in no hurry to get *anywhere*, other than away from his abusive father and the controlling Miss Watson. For Huck, floating downriver on a raft is an end in itself. But when Jim sets out from Jackson's island, his journey down the Mississippi is a means to an end, and the end is freedom. When Jim and Huck first spot the wreck of the steamboat *Walter Scott* in chapter 12, Jim smells trouble; he doesn't want to waste time searching the wreck. Huck, on the other hand, can think of nothing better than exploring it, especially since this would involve him in what Tom Sawyer would call "an adventure."[26] Despite the near fatal *contretemps* he experiences on board the steamboat, later Huck brags about how rich he and Jim have become as a consequence of their "adventures." But it is significant that Jim "said he didn't want no more adventures."[27] To Jim such adventures are too risky. He has a wary, potentially tragic view of life, borne, no doubt from his experiences as a slave.

[24] Twain, *HF*, 72.

[25] James M. Cox's and Forrest G. Robinson's insights concerning the "bad faith" between Jim and Huck attest convincingly to the fact that Huck's respect is by no means something that Jim can confidently rely on in all cases. Hence, Jim must use his wits to appeal to Huck on a variety of levels, including Huck's own racism. See James Cox, "A Hard Book to Take" in *One Hundred Years of Huckleberry Finn*, eds. Robert Sattelmeyer and J. Donald Crowley (Columbia: University of Missouri Press, 1985), 386-403; and Forest G. Robinson, "The Characterization of Jim in Huckleberry Finn," *Nineteenth Century Literatu*re 43 (1988): 361-391.

[26] Twain, *HF*, 57.

[27] Ibid., 64.

Commendably true to the slave narrative tradition of Pennington and Douglass, the first one-third of Mark Twain's novel introduces Jim as a black man with an adult's sense of goal-orientation, augmented by a fugitive slave's awareness of the desperateness of his rite of passage. But true to the boy's book tradition of *Tom Sawyer*, to which novel *Huckleberry Finn* is a sequel, Mark Twain created Huck with a boy's openness to and longing for all sorts of diversionary "adventures," that is, whatever excitement might pop up on the spur of the moment. In the first one-third of his novel, Mark Twain could reconcile Jim's priorities and Huck's, the adult slave narrative and the boy's book of adventures. But as Jim and Huck drift farther down the Mississippi and miss their chance to head up the Ohio River to freedom, Mark Twain could no longer write a slave narrative that was also a boy's adventure book. One had to give way to the other. Either the novel would be focused on Jim's urgent priority – from slavery to freedom by the most direct means available – or it would be a boy's book filled with comic misadventures of the kind that had been Clemens's literary stock-in-trade in previous books such as *The Innocents Abroad*, *A Tramp Abroad*, and *Tom Sawyer.*

Mark Twain didn't entitle his novel *The Adventures of Huckleberry Finn (Tom Sawyer's Comrade)* for nothing. The full title of the novel indicates that in the last two-thirds of the story the author put the slave narrative tradition behind him in favor of elaborating a series of Huck Finn's adventures. Jim and his quest for freedom are thrust farther and farther into the background. Once the two Arkansas conmen, the King and the Duke, commandeer the raft, Jim's role in the story becomes marginal and minor. Of course, both Jim and Huck know that they are drifting ever deeper into slave territory, necessitating increased vigilance and disguise. What is ominous, nevertheless, in the middle chapters of the novel, is Jim's failure to plead for his freedom agenda when he has the rare chance to do so. He registers a clandestine protest to Huck regarding the orneriness of this pair of pseudo-royalty, and he successfully lobbies the Duke to exchange the galling symbols of servitude – the ropes he must wear in his new public role as apprehended fugitive slave – for a more outlandish but less demeaning disguise as a "sick Arab," "harmless when not out of his head."[28] But beyond this Jim seems

[28] Ibid., 126.

as content as Huck just to drift aimlessly down the river while the Duke and the King call the shots. Perhaps we can understand Jim's behavior in the middle chapters of the novel as motivated simply by self-preservation. A savvy fugitive slave like Pennington would have agreed that when over-matched by the oppressor, it's wisest to keep your mouth shut and your eye on the prize – freedom. Nothing Jim does in the middle chapters of *Huckleberry Finn* contradicts this survival ethic. As long as the King and the Duke are in charge, it's not surprising that Jim keeps a low profile, doing nothing to antagonize these untrustworthy whites.

During the final one-third of the novel, however, when Jim is captured and held on the Phelps's farm, his behavior runs completely counter to what a Pennington or a Douglass would have done in the same situation. I'm not the first scholar or critic to notice the gross differences between Jim at the outset of his quest for freedom and Jim in the final chapters of the novel. In chapter 14 Jim totally rejects Huck's appeal to white privilege during their argument over whether Solomon was wise or not. Huck insists that Solomon was wise because the Widow Douglas herself – Huck's ultimate authority – told him so. Jim replies, "'I doan k'yer what de widder say, he warn't no wise man, nuther'" and thus underlines the fugitive's independence of mind.[29] Jim doesn't care what white authority says; he will stick to his own judgment of Solomon. However, in the last third of the book, Jim imprisoned on the Phelps farm seems reconciled to a perplexed dependency on Tom and Huck, despite the utter silliness of Tom's escape schemes. Huck writes: "Jim he couldn't see no sense in the most of it, but he allowed we was white folks and knowed better than him; so he was satisfied, and said he would do it all just as Tom said."[30]

Practically everything Jim does in the last chapters of the novel would appall James Pennington or Frederick Douglass. Jim becomes compliant and respectful towards Tom and Huck. Jim ignores his own needs and priorities. When Jim finally does complain about all Tom Sawyer's foolish schemes, Tom reproves him and the black man meekly knuckles under. The fugitive who once was determined to emancipate himself now is content to be an obedient

[29] Twain, *HF*, 65.
[30] Ibid., 126.

slave to a boy Jim starts calling "Mars Tom," that is, Master Tom. Jim even defers to his "Mars Tom" to tell him the right and proper way that Jim may escape.

If Jim were truly devoted to self-preservation, he might initially go along with Tom's fatuous games, perhaps to gain the white boy's confidence while making plans of his own. But as Tom manufactures more and more ridiculous tasks for Jim, the fugitive slave's well-being is increasingly jeopardized. The more Jim lets Tom delay his escape from the Phelps farm, the greater the likelihood that Jim will wake up one morning and find himself hoisted onto a wagon and shipped to New Orleans for sale. Jim's failure to express any sense of urgency about getting away before he gets sold is simply incomprehensible. When Jim finally does escape, during which time Tom gets shot in the leg, it is nothing short of astonishing for Jim to refuse to board the raft and complete his escape just because Tom got a minor flesh wound. Jim's self-sacrificing attentiveness to "Mars Tom" would make absolutely no sense to an African-American reader like Pennington or Douglass. Huck, obviously, could get a doctor for Tom, but, no, Jim refuses to leave Tom's side until the doctor, followed by white captors, arrives. Deeply moved by Jim's decision to sacrifice his freedom in order to help the doctor nurse Tom's wounds, Huck announces that Jim has proven that, regardless of his black exterior, "he was white inside."[31] Apparently, all Jim had to do to prove that was abandon his freedom quest in favor of loyalty to manipulative, narcissistic Tom Sawyer.

When Jim spurns his best chance for freedom and denies his own self-interest to nurse Tom, Mark Twain finally puts us on notice that *Adventures of Huckleberry Finn* has abandoned the slave narrative tradition totally. The first part of the novel celebrates a black man's *search* for freedom, and the middle part of the novel testifies to a black man's ability to *survive* for the sake of freedom. The best we can say about the last third of the novel is that it shows how much a black man can *endure* in the name of freedom. To be sure, the end of the book reveals that Mark Twain has no intention of actually denying Jim his freedom. In fact, it will be Tom who announces, when he is good and ready, of course, that Jim *is* free and actually *has been* free the whole time that Tom subjected him to the anxi-

[31] Ibid., 216.

ety and frustrations of imprisonment on the farm. This means that while Jim was dodging bullets during the highly dangerous escape engineered by Tom, the fugitive was risking his life for a freedom he already possessed, if only Tom had seen fit to inform him of it.

Why would Mark Twain have Tom keep Jim in the dark about his freedom? Mainly, I think, so that Mark Twain could have the farce at the end of his novel, a tedious sort of comedy to most readers of today, but one the author thought would entertain his late nineteenth-century readers as the novel reached a comic conclusion. The tedious high jinks end on a positive note when Jim finally gets his freedom, which was his goal from the start. However, from the standpoint of a Pennington or a Douglass, the comic ending of Mark Twain's novel would have been distinctly unfunny.

It's unfunny for at least two reasons. First, the humiliating role Jim has to play in Tom Sawyer's escape schemes is not funny. It's outrageous for an adult to be consistently lied to by a nearly egomaniacal boy for his own entertainment. Why, James W. C. Pennington would have asked, doesn't Jim assert himself when Tom's escape plans put Jim's life as well as his liberty in such jeopardy?

A second reason Mark Twain's ending is unfunny stems from Jim's reaction when he learns that, in fact, he was free the whole time that Tom was playing his escape games. Jim seems too dense to realize that the white boy he had been so devoted to had actually kept Jim enslaved through the whole plot and escape for no greater purpose than Tom's private self-indulgence. After Jim finds out all this, amazingly, he doesn't register the slightest bit of resentment. Instead, Jim is positively ecstatic over a paltry $40 payoff he gets from Tom for being such a patient prisoner. Early in the novel, Jim had a much different view of riches, declaring to Huck that he would be a rich man when he could own himself. But at the end of the novel, Jim has nothing but gratitude to Tom and Huck for the shoddy way they treated him.

What constitutes Mark Twain's final, irrevocable rejection of the slave narrative tradition is the revelation at the end of the novel that Jim is free, but *not by his own efforts*. This is, I contend, Mark Twain's ultimate joke at Jim's expense, worse than any of Huck's or Tom's jokes and silly games. The novel's disturbing climactic irony is that the fugitive slave will be allowed to *re*ceive – not achieve – his freedom, that is, through the unaccountable magnanimity of his dying former owner, Miss Watson. However, everything Jim did to attain his liberty turns out to have been pointless. By contrast, Pennington, Douglass, and the other famous fugitives of the slave narrative tradition attained their liberty through daring, courageous struggle, and triumph. Freed at the end of the novel, Jim's new status becomes clear when in the last chapter Tom confides to Huck and Jim his final scheme: "'le's all *three* slide out of here, one of these nights, and get an outfit, and go for howling adventures amongst the Indians.'"[32] We might expect an adult male to reply to Tom, "What do you mean, 'all three'"? We might expect Jim to laugh at the idea of joining these two white boys for more "howling adventures," Tom Sawyer-style. But Jim says nothing. He doesn't object to the plain implication that, in Tom's eyes, Jim is still another one of the boys, just waiting to follow Tom westward to Indian Territory. Indeed, we should not be surprised to hear Tom treating Jim as another boyhood chum at the end of the story. Jim's behavior through the last one third of the novel suggests that he has stopped thinking of himself as a grown man with a man's priorities and authority, despite the fact that, during their initial days on the river, Jim taught, advised, and protected Huck in fatherly ways, befitting an adult male's care for a boy irrespective of race or color. Jim's regression from man to boy as the novel develops may have been what lingered in Booker T. Washington's memory when, writing a tribute to Mark Twain in 1910, the Sage of Tuskegee called Jim the "poor, ignorant negro boy who accompanies the heroes of the story, Huckleberry Finn and Tom Sawyer, on a long journey down the Mississippi on a raft."[33] Washington's memory of the novel may have been faulty in the details, but his impression of Jim as a boy, not a man, indicates the tragically high price that Jim had to pay for freedom. To put it bluntly, the fugitive gets his freedom but loses his manhood, by which I mean his adulthood and his respectability as a black man.[34] Jim's demotion to one of the boys is borne out in *Tom*

[32] Twain, *HF*, 128.

[33] Booker T. Washington, "Tributes to Mark Twain," *North American Review* 191 (June 1910): 829.

[34] Mary Kemp Davis argues that Jim's manhood is rendered more problematic by the clothing he dons during his escape. Wearing a dress serves as "a visual emblem of his symbolic castration" (83). Mary Kemp Davis, "The Veil Rent in Twain: Degradation and Revelation in Adventures of Huckleberry Finn,"

Sawyer Abroad (1894) – the sequel to *Huckleberry Finn* – in which free Jim, unencumbered by a job, a family, or an adult mentality, teams up with Tom and Huck on a series of dreary adventures, this time in a hot-air balloon on an international course to nowhere.[35]

Scholars and critics have argued for well over a century about the ending of *Huckleberry Finn*. Ernest Hemingway said of the novel, "All modern American literature comes from one book by Mark Twain called 'Huckleberry Finn.' If you read it you must stop where the Nigger Jim is stolen from the boys. That is the real end. The rest is just cheating."[36] Hemingway's memory of the details of Mark Twain's novel appears to have been about as faulty as Booker T. Washington's, but I agree with Hemingway that the last part of the novel is "just cheating." Instead of "cheating" in the end, Hemingway would probably have demanded a much more tragic conclusion, perhaps the one that the scholar and critic John Seelye imagined when he re-wrote Clemens's novel in 1970 and published Huck's story as *The True Adventures of Huckleberry Finn*.[37] In Seelye's version of the story, Huck tells what really happened to him and Jim after Jim was captured and imprisoned on the Phelps farm. Huck says that he had planned to steal Jim from his captors, but before he could contact Jim about his plans, the fugitive made a break for his freedom by running to the river, weighed down by heavy chains, with bloodhounds and slave-catchers in hot pursuit. Huck had to watch Jim as he drowned in his chains in the Mississippi. This is clearly the worst-case scenario for Jim, but at least this tragic ending does not reduce Jim to a travesty or the tool of a white boy's narcissistic imagination. At least in Seeley's novel, Jim dies heroically committed to escape rather than returning to enslavement.

Satire or Evasion? Black Perspectives on Huckleberry Finn. eds. James S. Leonard, Thomas A. Tenney, and Thadious M. Davis (Durham, N.C.: Duke UP, 1992), 77-90.

35 One of Huck's remarks about Jim when he serves as pilot for the balloon summarizes Jim's devolution to the level of "boy" in *Tom Sawyer Abroad*. Faced with the prospect of an attack on the balloon by African lions, "Jim lost his head straight off – he always done it whenever he got excited or scared." *Tom Sawyer Abroad* (London: Chatto and Windus, 1894), 121.

36 Ernest Hemingway, *Green Hills of Africa* (New York: Scribner, 1935), 22.

37 John Seelye, *The True Adventures of Huckleberry Finn* (New York: Simon & Schuster, 1970).

What if James Pennington or Frederick Douglass had been given the opportunity to rewrite the ending of *The Adventures of Huckleberry Finn*? I think they probably would have chosen a comic, rather than tragic, ending, but nothing like the sort of comedy Mark Twain infused into his ending. The two real-life fugitives from slavery would not have let Jim receive a degrading freedom via the largesse of Tom Sawyer and Miss Watson. I think Pennington or Douglass would have decided to depict how Jim, accompanied and aided by Huck, ultimately gained his freedom. Mark Twain's imagination apparently could not admit of such an outcome, but the slave narrative tradition provides us dozens and dozens of personal histories that conclude with just such an outcome. Was it just too unlikely for a runaway slave as far South as mid-Arkansas (where the Phelps farm is) to make it all the way up the Mississippi to the free states? Not if you read the *Narrative of the Life and Adventures of Henry Bibb, an American Slave, Written by Himself*, published in the same year as *The Fugitive Blacksmith* and widely heralded in its own right.[38] Henry Bibb's fugitive slave narrative recounts his successful escape from Arkansas up the Mississippi and Ohio Rivers to freedom. So does William J. Anderson's 1857 fugitive slave narrative.[39] To be sure, most fugitives, among them Pennington and Douglass, who seized their freedom came from the border states – Maryland, Kentucky, and Virginia – not from the deep South. But the idea of an Arkansas slave's achieving his freedom through his own effort was certainly not unprecedented in the slave narrative tradition. It might seem far-fetched – but is it more far-fetched than the way that Mark Twain chose to conclude *his* novel?

Four months after the publication of *The Adventures of Huckleberry Finn*, Mark Twain wrote a letter to the dean of the law school at Yale University offering to pay the tuition of one of the first African Americans to be admitted to the Yale Law School. "We have ground the manhood out of them," Clemens observed,

38 Henry Bibb, *Narrative of the Life and Adventures of Henry Bibb, An American Slave, Written by Himself*, ed. Charles J. Heglar (1849; Madison: U of Wisconsin Press, 2001).

39 William J. Anderson, *Life and Narrative of William J. Anderson, Twenty-four years a Slave* (Chicago: 1857).

"& the shame is ours, not theirs, so we should pay for it."[40] This statement encapsulates an inconsistency in Mark Twain's thinking about social justice that is germane to the portrayal of Jim. Please note that the title of this essay is "James W. C. Pennington and Mark Twain: Slavery and the Moral Conscience of American Literature." Not the social conscience, but the moral conscience. Mark Twain's social conscience led him to support black men studying law at Yale University, an admirable thing for a white Southerner to do in 1885, a time when most Southern-born whites doubted that black men needed advanced education at all, let alone a degree to practice law. One could find much in Clemens's late essays and fiction to demonstrate that Mark Twain had an advanced and exemplary social conscience. But what does the fate of Jim in Clemens's novel say about the author's moral conscience, his view of Jim as an individual, not simply a runaway slave? Did Mark Twain really believe that black American males had had "the manhood ground out of them" by enslavement at the hands of whites? If so, how could those young black men who had gained admission to Yale Law School so distinguish themselves as to be qualified for admission in the first place? The notion that black men in 1885 had had "the manhood ground out of them" by whites put all black men, regardless of their individual preparation and achievement, into one class, that of victimized, needy, manhood-less males who required the support of guilty white progressives, especially white Southern progressives like Samuel Clemens. To expiate these white progressives' "shame," Clemens thought they – and he – ought to pay up, presumably to help black men recover their lost manhood. This line of thought, it seems to me, is symptomatic of a social conscience that can recognize injustice in broad, general, and highly racialized terms. But what Mark Twain wrote to the Yale dean does not speak well of Clemens's moral conscience, which, it appears, had a blind spot when it came to seeing those black Yale law students – or the fictional fugitive Jim – as *individual* adult African-Americans males, as men who, despite appalling racism, had not had their "manhood ground out of them," but who were striving independently to achieve the benefits of genuine freedom before Clemens decided to subsidize

[40] Guy Cardwell, *The Man Who Was Mark Twain* (New Haven: Yale UP, 1991), 194.

their educations. Like these real-life strivers, Jim, whose individuality Mark Twain made so strikingly impressive early in his novel, had a right to respectful treatment as a man, not to the point of idealization *a la* Stowe's near deification of Uncle Tom, but at least in ways that did not require Jim at the end of the novel to behave, in effect, like a black man who had had the manhood ground out of *him*.

James Pennington deserves the last word. In the preface to *The Fugitive Blacksmith*, Pennington denounced slavery for relegating the family histories of enslaved black men and women to their masters' property books. A former slave like himself, Pennington went on, could cite not "a single record to which he may appeal in vindication of his character, or honour." "Has a man no sense of honour because he was born a slave?" Pennington demanded. "Has he no need of character?"[41] I wish Mark Twain had remembered these words from *The Fugitive Blacksmith*, and not just Pennington's wonderful smallpox lie. If the white author had remembered that a fugitive or former slave had a very real "need of character" in literature, as well as in life, perhaps Clemens's moral conscience would have led him to endow the fugitive Jim with as much character at the end of *Huckleberry Finn* as Jim possessed when he launched his journey for freedom early in the novel. If Mark Twain had seen fit to honor Jim's pride, dignity, and manhood throughout the novel, rather than sacrificing those qualities for the amusement of whites, there would have been no need for "cheating" in order to bring *Huckleberry Finn* to a satisfactory conclusion. And Mark Twain's novel would live today as a monument to character, not just Huck's but Jim's as well.

[41] Pennington, *The Fugitive Blacksmith*, xii